T0349986

Praise for *Building a Millionaire Mindset*

"The minute I met Johnny Wimbrey, I knew he was a 'person of interest.' Incredible connectivity, incredible people skills, and an incredible story that I could relate to. I highly recommend anything he writes, speaks on, or trains on as he is a person that, when I'm with him, I feel better about me. Becoming a millionaire starts with one thing: a *decision* to go. This book gives you the *mindset* and *tool set* necessary to becoming a millionaire. Life will be better when you get to the other side of the financial puzzle. Nobody does it better than Johnny—not only telling you how to do but actually doing it."

—MICHAEL BURT, America's Coach
and author of 16 books

"If you are ready to transform your life and your bank account the way Johnny has done, read this book! Within these pages, you will awaken the millionaire mindset within you and find yourself stretching and growing into the person that you were designed to be. The strategies, principles, and truths that Johnny shares are beyond anything you have encountered before. Johnny is a dedicated husband and father, and he's a person who I believe is living the calling on his life—being a voice of transformation. We are all fortunate that he's willing to share what he's learned with the world. Congratulations on investing in yourself and for getting out of your head and into your greatness by reading *Building a Millionaire Mindset*."

—LES BROWN, Emmy Award–winning
speaker, trainer, and author

"I would like to congratulate Johnny on this incredible new book. He has always had a heart to reach people in a positive way and empower them to make their lives better, and that's what I love most about him. His message has remained the same and has not changed over the years. Trust God, love your family, and bet on yourself. He has always understood how to accomplish this the right way, which includes mentors and wise counsel and surrounding yourself with people who share the same goals. The only thing I believe he has not mastered is golf, and if he ever got serious about it, I would probably be in trouble. My prayer is that Johnny continues to do what God has called him to do. When you are doing God's work, it's never easy, but it's always worth it. God bless."

—LARRY BROWN, JR., former
NFL football player and
MVP of Super Bowl XXX

"Johnny Wimbrey has been a friend and a mentor of mine for a number of years. His transformation from street life to being a first-generation millionaire, coupled with his ability to teach us how to do the same, is nothing short of remarkable! This book teaches the mindset to not only gain success but also to maintain and sustain generational success, which is something I wish I had had access to as a professional athlete. Having access to Johnny has expanded my mindset to say the least. Your transformation can happen as well if you read and apply these pillars! God bless."

—RAY CROCKETT, two-time Super Bowl
champion, author, motivational speaker,
and entrepreneur

"Johnny Wimbrey is the message that he brings! His personal story of tragedy to triumph makes him the leading authority when it comes to teaching anyone who has a burning desire to master the mindset of a first-generation millionaire. This book is a must-read for anyone who wants to have a breakout season that leads to a lifestyle of perpetual successes!"

—TED NUYTEN, CEO of Business
For Home (businessforhome.org)

"The right mindset is critical to increase your wealth. Johnny Wimbrey not only has built a mindset that has enriched him, but with *Building a Millionaire Mindset*, he has also laid out the raw mental materials for readers to learn how to build a mindset that will increase their wealth exponentially."

—DEVON FRANKLIN, *New York Times*
bestselling author, Hollywood producer,
and motivational speaker

"I know firsthand that massive success is the evidence of extraordinary coaching. This book is a game changer for anyone who wants to build a winner's mindset. There is no question that all victories mentally begin within. Generational passed-on wealth is one of the greatest championship games of my life. When it comes to *Building a Millionaire Mindset*, Johnny's step-by-step playbook is an absolute must-read!"

—EMMITT SMITH, former NFL player and
three-time Super Bowl champion

"Often there seems to be an insurmountable gulf between 'haves' and the 'have-nots'; between the successful and the success seekers. What I like about Johnny Wimbrey's *Building a*

Millionaire Mindset is that it has the unique advantage of being written by an author who has lived on both sides of the track. Many people can share mindsets, but what is unique is that Johnny can teach lofty ideas in attainable language. Don't miss this opportunity to hear 'their' talk in 'your' language!"

—T. D. JAKES SR., author of several *New York Times* bestsellers, CEO of TDJ Enterprises, and Pastor at The Potter's House of Dallas

"In *Building a Millionaire Mindset*, Johnny Wimbrey shows you how he went from being the son of a trashman to being a first-generation millionaire and how you can too. He'll teach you to value yourself, have faith in yourself, and commit to yourself all the way. Johnny builds millionaires, and now it's your turn!"

—EVAN CARMICHAEL, entrepreneur, author, speaker, influencer, dreamer, and #Believer

"Johnny is the real deal. I've known him for years, and I have seen how he operates everywhere from business meetings to Sundays with his family. He knows how to lead a conversation, command a room, and make his mind known on paper. Johnny always speaks from the heart because he has lived every single lesson he teaches. There is truth in his words because there is a unique Johnny Wimbrey story behind every piece of advice he gives. This book is a testament to his journey as a man who has broken the cycle in his family and lives the life of a true first-generation millionaire."

—JAN MILLER, cofounder of Dupree Miller, the leading nonfiction literary agency in the world, representing clients such as Tony Robbins, Dr. Phil, and Joel Osteen

"Johnny Wimbrey has done so much to change the trajectory and course of his life and that of his family and others whom he has worked with. Johnny has the ability to systematically show you through hard work, confidence, diligence, and a mentality of success the steps that you will need for daily, weekly, and lifelong progress to success and prosperity. His ability to overcome any obstacle put in his way shows you his determination and focus with anything he does. This book will help change your life and guide you to your next level."

—Nancy Lieberman, NBA Hall of Famer
and founder of Nancy Lieberman Charities

"I personally had a front row seat watching Johnny Wimbrey go from young, broke, and hopeful to young, rich, and free. *Building a Millionaire Mindset* is a must-read if you ever want to know the principles of building wealth. Johnny will teach you how to start from where you are and become the first millionaire in your family."

—Holton Buggs, millionaire coach
and CEO of iBuumerang

"Johnny Wimbrey is a fantastic role model for people who think that their hardships are too much to create greatness in their lives. *Building a Millionaire Mindset* brilliantly provides the road map to not only help overcome any obstacles in your way but also build a foundation that will help you create wealth and have the proper mental framework to keep it for generations."

—Tim Storey, author, motivational
speaker, and life coach to many,
including Oprah Winfrey

BUILDING A MILLIONAIRE MINDSET

BUILDING A MILLIONAIRE MINDSET

HOW TO USE THE PILLARS OF ENTREPRENEURSHIP TO GAIN, MAINTAIN, **AND SUSTAIN LONG-LASTING WEALTH**

JOHNNY WIMBREY

NEW YORK   CHICAGO   SAN FRANCISCO   ATHENS   LONDON   MADRID
MEXICO CITY   MILAN   NEW   DELHI   SINGAPORE   SYDNEY   TORONTO

3 4 5 6 7 8 9   LCR   25 24 23 22

ISBN: 978-1-260-47507-4
MHID: 1-260-47507-7

e-ISBN: 978-1-260-47508-1
e-MHID: 1-260-47508-5

Design by Lee Fukui and Mauna Eichner

Library of Congress Cataloging-in-Publication Data

Names: Wimbrey, Johnny, author.
Title: Building a millionaire mindset : how to use the pillars of
   entrepreneurship to gain, maintain, and sustain long-lasting wealth /
   Johnny Wimbrey.
Description: New York City : McGraw Hill, 2020. | Includes bibliographical
   references and index.
Identifiers: LCCN 2020029645 (print) | LCCN 2020029646 (ebook) |
   ISBN
   9781260475074 (hardback) | ISBN 9781260475081 (ebook)
Subjects: LCSH: Creative ability in business. | Success—Psychological
   aspects. | Entrepreneurship—Technological innovations. | Success in
   business.
Classification: LCC HD53 .W566 2020 (print) | LCC HD53 (ebook) |
   DDC
   658.4/21—dc23
LC record available at https://lccn.loc.gov/2020029645
LC ebook record available at https://lccn.loc.gov/2020029646

McGraw Hill books are available at special quantity discounts to use as premiums and sales promotions or for use in corporate training programs. To contact a representative, please visit the Contact Us pages at www.mhprofessional.com.

Dedication

To my father, who will be forever missed . . .

. . . I dedicate this book in its entirety to you.

In the midst of my writing this book, Daddy, on September 1, 2019, you transitioned to your eternal resting place, passing the torch to all your children as the next generation of Wimbrey descendants. It is my prayer that in my own years as a grandfather, my children, Psalms Noel, Hannah Joél, and Honor Montrel, will be as honored as I am to carry the "Wimbrey Legacy" to far higher heights.

The reason I wrote this book was you, Daddy. When I was a young boy around the age of 12, you uttered four words that seemed so simple at the time, not knowing that over a decade later those four words would ultimately become the foundation of my global message.*

As a sanitation worker or "trash-man," as you would call yourself, you worked very early hours. Typically, when my brothers and I came home from school, you would be outside in the yard drinking, playing dominoes, and grilling BBQ, usually shirtless with a towel around your neck. Old-school music

---

* Reader, as I tell you this story, I want you to imagine my father as Samuel L. Jackson's character from the movie *Pulp Fiction*. Without exaggeration, this was my father's temperament.

would be playing in the background as we would walk up to the yard every afternoon. As I write this, I remember it as if it were yesterday.

It was report card day, and I was nervous. It was mandatory that we all bring our report cards straight to you and place them in your hands after school, before we could do anything else. The reason I was nervous was because—as everyone who knew you knows—you had zero filter. You would always say the first thing that popped into your head. Walking home from school on this particular afternoon, I could hear you from the next block over talking smack and making people laugh as usual. You weren't alone. All I could think of as I walked up to the house was that I was about to be center stage in an unpredictable show in front of the company.

Because it was mandatory, I knew that I had to talk to each individual adult in my presence, hand you my report card, and then wait. I knew that you would go straight to my citizenship grades first and then check over my academic grades—something you didn't have to do with my siblings. That day, I knew what was coming.

My citizenship grade was no surprise: Needs Improvement. "Talks too much," the note said. Looking back now as an adult, I am extremely impressed how you never really killed my personality (*talking too much*) with discipline. You would just shrug it off, mutter under your breath, "Yup, this boy talks too much," and just keep going. You knew that I worked hard where it mattered. Just a few years before this report card, I had failed the second grade, and I had to repeat it. But once my brothers and I moved back in with you, my grades were always at the top percent of my class. I did not have any failing grades, but this particular report card had a big, ugly C on it. A first for me since you started taking care of us.

You handed my report card back to me and without looking at me you said, "C? Anyone can be average." Those four words "Anyone can be average" would ultimately be the foundational pillar that would drive me to becoming a first-generation millionaire. Daddy, you are the reason that I hate to be associated with anything close to average. That afternoon, as you handed that report card back to me, you ignited within me the mindset of a first-generation millionaire. That's why I dedicate this book to you.

Yep, a *trash-man* told me, "Anyone can be average." This idea gave birth to the mindset that would lead me to become the man I am today.

To my mother, Phyllis, and my stepfather, Tim; to my stepmother, Joyce; to my siblings from youngest to eldest, my baby sister, Ronnietta, and older brothers, Willie, Lawrence, Jr., and Corey—I love you with all my heart, and I am extremely grateful for your love and protection.

To my wife and best friend, Crystal Monique Wimbrey, everything I do is for you and our children: Psalms, Hannah, Honor, and all the Wimbrey descendants yet to come long after I am gone, I love you all with every breath I breathe and beyond.

Contents

PART I

PREPARATION VERSUS IMPROVISATION

PART II
VISION VERSUS ILLUSION

PART III
FRIENDS VERSUS FOES

PART IV
INSPECT WHAT YOU EXPECT

PART V
EXECUTE VERSUS EXCUSE

Foreword

What does it take to be a success in today's unprecedented economic climate? Is it skill, determination, grit, knowledge?

Sure, those are all key elements of success, but to truly make it today, and in the future, you have to have much more. You need to have the *millionaire mindset*.

Many years ago, I received a phone call from a young man who told me that he wanted to train with me and to learn how to do what I do. I wasn't flattered. I know there are millions of people who want to change the world with their voices, and I receive countless requests to train speakers all the time.

I listened to his story and told him that I was willing to teach him, but it wouldn't be easy, and it would require a substantial financial investment. He told me that he didn't have the money at the time but he would get it.

Afterward, I forgot about the conversation, but within one week's time, I received the follow-up call that would change not only Johnny Wimbrey's life but my life too!

Johnny converted that investment in training with me to millions of dollars and influence around the world. He has literally built an empire where he now teaches others how to dream and become the greatest versions of themselves.

What is it about Johnny that makes him unique? Here's a guy who was literally raised by the streets who has gone on to become a revered thought leader and elite coach in the personal development world.

Johnny likes to say, he went "from the hood to doing good!"

How did he do it? He beat the seemingly insurmountable odds and kept going when so many others would have tucked their tails and run. What made him so unstoppable?

It was by using the principles in *Building a Millionaire Mindset*.

If you are ready to transform your life and your bank account the way Johnny has done, read this book!

Within these pages, you will awaken the millionaire mindset within you and find yourself stretching and growing into the person that you were designed to be.

The strategies, principles, and truths that Johnny shares are beyond anything you have encountered before.

Johnny is a dedicated husband and father, and he's a person who I believe is living the calling on his life—being a voice of transformation. We are all fortunate that he's willing to share what he's learned with the world.

Congratulations on investing in yourself and for getting out of your head and into your greatness by reading *Building a Millionaire Mindset*.

LES BROWN
Emmy Award–winning
speaker, trainer, author

Acknowledgments

Thank you to Crystal Wimbrey and my family. I am forever grateful for your unconditional love and support.

Sincere gratitude to Carol Fields, Derek Williams, and my team at Wimbrey Training Systems for unmeasured time, dedication, and teamwork in making this possible.

Special thanks to Deepa Chungi for helping formulate the book.

And thank you to 2 Market Media and Steve Carlis for believing in my vision and supporting my every step in this process.

And an enormous thank you to McGraw Hill for the opportunity to publish this.

Introduction

There have been no millionaires before me with the last name Wimbrey. I am the first one. My father was a trashman. He was a very hard worker; all I saw in him was hard work. He was not a millionaire, but my father's mindset to expose my siblings and me to the multimillion-dollar homes from his sanitation truck route had a direct bearing on my vision, hunger, and passion for massive increase.

Vision is created only by exposure, and whether he knew it or not, my father teed up my vision exactly the way golfers tee up their golf ball for a better view and advantage to swing for distance and momentum. I don't know anyone on either the black or white sides of my family who had a million in the bank when they died. Growing up, I never expected an inheritance or looked forward to getting access to a trust fund when I turned 18. Nothing like that existed for me. But it will for my children because the book you are about to read was written by a true, genuine, first-generation millionaire.

However, I want to take a step back from the money for a moment. First, I want to talk about your character. Becoming successful—becoming that first-generation millionaire in your family—has everything to do with the *character* you bring to the table. Before you can even start thinking about the money, the success, or the clout, first you must—*must*—have a conversation with your character. Your true character, the person you are when it is just you and you. **Without the right character in place and without knowing who you are and what you are capable of, you will never achieve and maintain true success.**

True success should begin within. You make the success! The success should never make you. This is why the millionaire mindset must begin from within, so that you not only *gain* but also *maintain* and *sustain* that which leads to generational wealth.

That is what this book is about. It is not about closing sales or how to run a multimillion-dollar company or how to cash in on your side hustle so you can quit your day job. **This book is about building the character you need in order to succeed.** I firmly believe that people who continuously work to develop their *internal* success of personal character will ultimately have many *external* successes.

Almost every millionaire I've helped coach or train, every personal business client I've coached, and every person I've mentored was broke and hungry for a greater life when I met him or her. Today, many of them are worth millions not because of their business acumen or their ability to convince the people they meet to buy something. No. It's because I have ingrained in them the exact millionaire mindset that has been ingrained in me, the three most important keys they need in order to have the character of a first-generation millionaire. If you don't build these keys—these mental muscles—and exercise them constantly, your success will be miniscule and fleeting.

Before you start flipping through the book and rushing to Pillar 1, ask yourself if you have the desire to disrupt the past to create a new you. There are no shortcuts here to obtain the true mindset of a first-generation millionaire. Absolutely no cutting corners. There is no cheating. This is your life. *You* must do the work.

To get started, answer the following questions:

- Do you have the drive to transform yourself into a person who knows for a fact that you will not die working but rather, die watching your work lead to generational wealth?

- Will you grant yourself permission to implement a foundational vision statement that says the following: "I will not leave debt to my children and my children's children, but rather I will leave generational wealth. My family members will be able to live off of my work, which will tee them up for their personal works even if their paths are totally different."

If you answered yes to one or both of those questions, you are ready to embrace the mindset of a first-generation millionaire. Duplicating the millionaire mindset is far greater than duplicating an industry or product. Products and industries change and can even die, but the millionaire mindset is designed to last for generations. Are you ready to be the person in your family who finally creates lasting wealth? If so, you must be ready to learn about yourself, to allow yourself to discover things that you thought you had forgotten or hidden away, to transform into someone who has the character of a first-generation millionaire. If you truly have a burning desire to implement this mindset and take on the assignment of becoming a first-generation millionaire, then I invite you to read on.

The three keys essential to the character of every first-generation millionaire I know are these:

Value: Do you value yourself and your abilities? If you truly want to succeed in life with a solid foundation, first you need to understand and appreciate your personal value. Just as every human being's thumbprint and DNA are unique, there is something unique about you that only you were designed to leave on this planet before you depart.

All of your personal answers will be uncovered and revealed page by page during your journey of completing this book. Your personal value is directly linked to the personal confidence and posture that you bring to any conversation, deal, or presentation. Confidence and posture show up only when you can truly identify and walk in your God-given value. The world benefits for many generations from those who tap into their true personal value.

Faith: Do you have faith in *yourself*? Not in your ideas. Not in your team. Not in your product. Not in your website. Not even in your family. In *yourself*. When things go south, when your best employees quit, or when your product gets trumped in the marketplace, do you have faith that you will be able to start from scratch and create success all over again? You must have faith in yourself and your abilities. Otherwise, the very first wave will wash you away completely.

Those who consistently build faith in themselves will ultimately tap into a much higher degree of personal purpose. I am going to expose you to the exact practices I use even to this day to build my faith in myself. I was born in poverty, and my first memory is of when I was homeless and living in a shelter for battered women. The most vivid memories after that are when I failed the second grade and when I had a teenage felony arrest. These are just a few of the many obstacles that I will share with you in this book. But through it all, I still had faith. I decided at the age of 20 that my past would not dictate my future! That mindset alone was and has been one of my foundational faith keys that have led me to become the man I am today.

Commitment: Do you have the commitment to take this all the way? Are you honest enough with yourself to ensure that you will give this effort 100 percent of your energy 100 percent of the time? Without commitment, quitting is too easy. Without commitment, you will never be a first-generation millionaire.

Think of wealth mastery and the millionaire mindset as a house you want to renovate. You can change the doors, redo the windows, and add a garage, but there are some walls that your contractor will tell you that you cannot touch. These walls are integral to the structure of the house. Without them, everything will start to crumble. These three keys—value, faith, and commitment—are like those walls. The house was built around them. You are no different. You can't play with them, you can't negotiate with them, and you can't succeed without them.

Let's talk about **value**. When I was about 25 years old, I was asked to speak at a prominent church. I wasn't asked to speak to leadership or the congregation but to the leaders' children. The youth of the church. Now, I am always ten toes down, ready for anything, when talking to young people. I was the troublemaker and class clown when I was young, and I looked up to those people who came to speak to me, so I am always looking for my past self in the crowd when I am speaking to young people. I want to be able to handle him or her before he or she jumps.

But this crowd was different. These weren't kids who were forced to be there, rolling their eyes from the get-go. This audience was made up of the children of the leaders we all respect. They were being exposed to phenomenal teachings every day. They were constantly surrounded by greatness. It was in their blood. I had to improve on what they already knew, so the topic I chose that day was something all children should hear about starting from a young age. I spoke to them about their personal value.

I started my speech by pulling out a hundred-dollar bill. I showed it to them and asked, "How much is this worth?" They said it was worth a hundred dollars. I folded it in half and asked them again, "How much is this worth?" Again, they said it was worth a hundred dollars. I asked them why the value didn't change when I folded the bill, and they told me, "Even folded, it is still worth a hundred dollars."

"What if I fold it again?" I asked. Now it was a quarter of what it once was, but the children said it still worth a hundred dollars. "You're telling me that if I decrease the size and visibility to a *quarter* of what it was, that the value is still there?" That was when they started looking at me like I was crazy.

"*Yes!*" they all screamed.

"What if I fold it *again*? What if I crumple it up and throw it on the ground? What if it gets mud all over it and it looks like garbage? What if I step on it? Then what is it worth?"

"Brother Johnny," they shouted back, "it's still worth a hundred dollars!"

With emotions extremely high, I enthusiastically asked, "So, you're telling me that as long as it stays intact—as long as I can smooth it out, rinse it off, make it straight—there is nothing I can do to this piece of paper to cause it to lose its value?" They all nodded back at me. Then I asked them, "What would you do if someone stepped on your dreams? Crumpled up your ambitions and aspirations? Folded you in half? Mentally, emotionally? Would you lose your value?" Silence. Then I asked them, "How can this man-made object, this bill made of paper, have more value than you, a God-made object?"

You *must* value yourself or you will never be a first-generation millionaire. People from any bloodline who have ever accomplished something that has never been done before can always trace that accomplishment back to their breakthrough in understanding and accepting their personal value. It is one of the core characteristics you need to succeed on this journey. If people try to fold you in half, crumple you up, or step on you—*and they will*—you must be sure that nothing and nobody has the ability to take away your value. Knowing this as a certainty and exercising this value is something I learned from a young age.

This book will show you how to internalize that feeling and use it to empower yourself as you work to accumulate your first million and beyond.

The second key is **faith**. I'm not talking about your faith in God. I'm talking about your faith in *yourself.* Where is that faith in yourself? In your abilities? In your drive? Before you answer those questions, think about the last chair you sat in; perhaps the one you are sitting in right now. When you went to sit down, you didn't check the chair first. You simply walked up to it and sat. When you go to a restaurant or to see a play, you don't inspect the chair in which you are about to sit. You just sit. You have faith that the chair will hold you up. Now, do you have that same faith in yourself? Or do you say to yourself, "What if I call this person and he or she says no? It's going to hurt my feelings." Or, "What if my employees don't think I know what I am doing?"

You didn't talk to the chair about being there for you, about doing its job, about not letting you down. But when you have to do the thing that needs to be done, do you start asking yourself if it's even possible? If so, *why?* Why do you have more faith in the chair than you do in your own ability to be a first-generation millionaire? You *must* have faith in yourself or you will never succeed. It's a fact that I have proven over and over again.

When presented with an opportunity to expand my team, I got on a plane to go to South Africa on my own dime, to Australia on my own dime, to London on my own dime. My company didn't want to send me. The company's leaders didn't want to take the risk; they didn't want to invest in something that was not a sure thing. But I had faith in myself. I knew that if I went to those places, I could build the relationships, build the partnerships, and create something out of nothing. I had faith that the very same executives and partners who stayed behind would soon see what I was capable of achieving and follow me across continents. I want you to have that same faith in yourself. Take your faith that a man-made chair will hold you up, and apply that faith to yourself. Only when you are able to do this will you have what it takes to be a first-generation millionaire.

Alongside value and faith, there is **commitment**. When I say "commitment," I mean *your* definition of being committed, not someone else's. Commitment requires a personal connection to an assignment. If you are working on something that you cannot create a genuine connection to, that should be your first red flag. What you are working on now is someone else's assignment. It's not yours.

That said, when you are first starting out, the best way to understand the idea of commitment is to become a part of other people's commitment to *their* assignment for a season. By working on others' commitment, you can expose yourself to new ideas, hone your skills, and figure out what it is that you want your own commitment to be. You can find your own value in raising up their work. By working with other people initially, you can learn about what you love and put your stamp on something as you work on it. Use these experiences as a jumping off point before you commit to a project that really speaks to what you love and what you are good at.

You *know* what you are masterful at—everyone is masterful at something. But when you are blessed and gifted in a certain area, it's so easy to hide behind someone else's definition of greatness. Even if you know better. Just because someone says you are the best salesperson, promoter, or marketing mind he or she has ever seen, that doesn't mean that it is *your* best. I am at the top of my field. I have been speaking in front of hundreds of thousands of people every year for well over a decade now. My companies generate nine figures a year in global production. But that is still not *my* best. I am writing this book because I want to commit to what I am called to do and help you do the same.

To understand your commitment to your goal, imagine a vending machine. If you want some chips but you feel like eating only half the bag, you still have to put in the whole dollar. The machine will never give you half the chips for 50 cents. If you put in 50 cents, the machine will give you *nothing*. As a matter of fact, just like life, it will reject your efforts and spit your coins back out. You need to commit to the whole bag. You need to put in 100 percent, the whole dollar. There is no negotiation.

You may *say* you want to be a first-generation millionaire, but then you try to negotiate your life away. You don't commit to waking up two hours early to chase leads and do research. You don't stay at work late to follow up on calls and ideas. You just want to put in that 50 cents and get that half bag of chips.

This is where I tell you to stop that behavior now. Before you read any further, you *must* commit to the whole bag. You simply cannot negotiate commitment if you want to be a first-generation millionaire. Negotiate your desire to have everyone like you. Negotiate what you are OK with when others talk about you behind your back. But never negotiate your commitment to this journey. You will not become a first-generation millionaire without first committing to it 100 percent.

If you know that you cannot give everything you have to these three keys—value, faith, and commitment—stop reading now, and put this book away until you can make that personal commitment, or give this book to someone you care about who is hungry and has a burning desire to be that breakout generation. This book is designed for those who want to awaken the giant that lives within. This book is for those who will commit to the commitment!

These keys will be the foundation of your character, which will bring you that success and allow you to *keep it*. The character that will pick you up when you fall. The character that you will pass on to your children's children so they can continue on this path.

If you are obsessed with the numbers in your bank statement, your rank in a company, or the amount of sales you bring but you do *not* think about your character, you will fail. I can give you all the information you need on how to close a sale, pitch to investors, or run a business, but it won't mean *anything* unless you invest in your character first. This book is your first step toward investing in your own character. These three keys will carry you on this journey to being a first-generation millionaire.

Remember that hundred-dollar bill that keeps its value, no matter what. Remember that man-made chair in which you have so much faith. Remember that vending machine that demands you go all in or get nothing. If you truly want to have this, to build this, to be a first-generation millionaire, you need to have faith in yourself. You have to value what you bring to the table. And you have to commit to your cause. This book is not for just anyone and everyone. It is for the people who are willing to change the **trajectory** of their lives. It is for those who are ready to change who they are in order to take the next step—those who are willing to do the work and own the person they will become.

This book is your road map to greatness. Do the work. Lock it up. Make it happen for your family and yourself. Everything you do from now on is in your control. Don't let anyone tell you otherwise.

With these keys and the lessons from the journey we are about to embark on together, success is standing right in front of you. Build and maintain that true character—who you are when it is just you and yourself. Laying this foundation is the first step to becoming a first-generation millionaire. Let's get started.

BUILDING A MILLIONAIRE MINDSET

Participating in Your Own Rescue

f you want to be that first-generation millionaire, if you want to succeed, if you want to reap the benefits of your hard work, you *must* be willing at all costs to participate in your own rescue. You must have the mindset of a **winner**. Not a whiner. What's the difference? Let me tell you a story.

It was early fall of 1995. I was 20 years old. I had finished my degree in acting school and was focused on getting a job that would allow me to go to auditions. Becoming a sales rep seemed like the obvious choice; I could control my schedule and set my own hours. To meet that goal, I started working in the sales department of a national insurance agency. In Texas, you can get a temporary 90-day insurance license, mainly to try it out to see if you like it enough to stay in the industry. At the end of the

90-day trial period, you take the test to get your permanent license. By the end of *my* trial period, I was one of the highest-earning agents in the United States. Out of thousands of licensed agents, as a temporary licensed agent, I had risen to the top 50 agents in just 90 days; deciding whether to take the test and get my official license was not difficult at all.

After failing the test twice, I finally passed the test on my third go-around with a just-passing grade of 72. That's 3 points over failure, but it was enough! I had paid for my own classes, and I had paid for the test three times in less than four weeks. This was me participating in my own rescue, but this was just the beginning. The unknown massive rejection was still awaiting just around the corner.

Still superexcited that I had passed the test, I mailed in my application and test results, and then I waited for my license to arrive. Finally! This was my major reset button on life. This was my foundational point of personal redemption, from homelessness to failing in school to that teenage felony arrest. I was now a professional licensed insurance agent for the state of Texas. Eagerly I awaited for what seemed like months, and a week later, a letter from the Texas Department of Insurance came in the mail. I saw the postmark and return address and actually jumped up and down. I was so excited to start the next phase of my life. I felt like a kid on Christmas morning. As I ripped open the envelope and unfolded the letter, my smile faded and my unwrapped Christmas present turned into an obituary. The words floated off of the paper.

"Sorry to inform you."

"You cannot represent the state of Texas."

"Felony arrest."

My past—my teenage mistakes—had come back to haunt me. I had to make a decision. I could wallow. I could yell about how I was trying to build something for myself and my girlfriend, Crystal. I could scream about how "The Man" wasn't letting me climb out of my old life. I could sit there and be a whiner. Or I could stand up and be a winner. I could take responsibility. I knew I deserved what I got based on the decisions I had made. I actually started talking to the letter. "I *do* have a felony arrest. I *know* I did it. It's only by God's grace and mercy that I am alive and not in prison." I could own my past or bury it. I decided to own it.

I didn't mope. I didn't punch a wall. I didn't get drunk with my friends. Right then and there, I decided to kick down the door to the rest of my life. I was on fire. I had just turned 21. I had just graduated with a performing arts degree with a major in acting. And now the state of Texas was telling me no? Nope. Not today! As William Ward said, "Adversity causes some to break, but it causes others to become record breakers." I was going to break or become a record breaker.

Instantly my inner giant—my inner winner—woke up. In that moment, I decided I would exercise *faith*, *commitment*, and *value* simultaneously. I knew in my heart that this decision on whether to accept failure or participate in my own rescue would literally make or break my future in my career as a licensed insurance agent. With the letter still burning in my hand, I called the county clerk at the courthouse in Fort Worth, Texas. It was the exact courthouse that had lifted my felony arrest to a lowercase misdemeanor. I was painfully aware that it was unlikely the clerk would even take my call, but he did. To my surprise, the clerk remembered me, and so did Judge Wayne Salvant.

"Listen. I was in your court about a year ago, and I am really working to get my life on track. I know that my felony was dropped to a class C misdemeanor. If possible, can you please, *please*, write a letter on my behalf simply stating *anything* that will give me another chance?" To my surprise, they wrote the letter on my behalf. No promises, no guarantees, and no expectations. Just a simple letter.

A week later, I got another envelope in the mail. It wasn't a letter from the courthouse. It was in the same sized envelope as before, and it looked exactly like the enveloped I had opened weeks before that had carried my denial letter. I did not open the letter as fast as I had done previously. I prayed to God first. I took a moment to reflect. I made a personal decision that whatever was in this envelope was what I deserved and what I had earned. I knew in that moment that I would take personal ownership of that reality. I took a breath and opened the letter. To my surprise, there was no letter, there was no explanation. It was only my license. I was official! Johnny Dewayne Wimbrey, Health & Life Insurance Agent, Texas Department of Insurance. This single piece of paper represented my personal vindication, my reset button on life. I went on to become one of the top insurance agents in the nation within nine months. Before I was 25, I would earn a regional vice president contract enabling me to recruit and train agents for multiple territories in the United States.

Why did I get my license? Because I had the mindset of a winner. The only reason I got my license was because I took that next step. **I participated in my own rescue.** This is what I want you to focus on. If you want to be a winner, I challenge you to participate in your rescue. Take that extra step.

I could have gotten really pissed *off* at the state of Texas, but the whole episode actually *pissed me on*. Getting *pissed off* makes a person feel empowered, but in reality, it is an average personality attribute that even toddlers have. Getting pissed off is not a gift, and it's not a talent. It just means you are a normal, everyday human being. *Success* and *normal* are oxymorons. Whiners are normal. Winners are not! I want you to stay in the land of the winner, to run away from being a whiner. You have to take action if you want to participate in your own rescue. I could have sat and wallowed when I got that first letter, but I refused to. Where would I be now if I had never picked up the phone and called the courthouse? I can't even imagine all the paths I never would have taken if I had just given up.

You are already participating in your own rescue by reading this book. Reading even to this point means you are committed to seeing yourself through this journey. But remember, this is not one of those books that you will finish in a day and never refer to again. As you go through this process, understand that this is not a race. I want you to appreciate the process just as much as you will the results. Keep track of the big moments and the big breakthroughs, and document them. Keep a journal, and write down how you feel when each of those big moments hits you. I want you to form an emotional connection with the high (and low) points of this journey. Keep track of your progress as you go along, and come back to your notes after a year, or two, or three. Write notes in the margins, and highlight the parts that really speak to you. This book will be your companion for years to come.

Exercises like this will help you internalize the ideas in this book so that they stick with you, and we will keep coming back to **this idea of participating in your own rescue** so that sticks too.

This is important because I've seen countless people wander away from their own rescue when things got hard or uncomfortable. Don't be one of those people. Stay the course! Warning signs that you have stopped participating in your own rescue are these:

- **Acting like victims:** Victims spend their time and precious energy blaming their problems on others and on what is going wrong around them, instead of thinking of and actively trying to find ways to fix things. Anyone can be a victim, but a true champion focuses on the solution or how to respond to this experience to become bigger and more powerful.

- **Focusing on obstacles rather than opportunities:** Obstacles are everywhere. They are obvious and easy to find, so if you focus on them, you will only expand them. Instead, channel that focus and your energy on finding *opportunities*. Seek them out under rocks and in trees. They may be harder to find, but they will flourish under your attention.

- **Arguing for your limitations rather than your abilities:** When you focus on limitations (such as "I grew up poor" or "I have been raising my kids for eight years, so no one will hire me now"), you are too distracted to see your abilities, which are much more important. Focusing on your abilities would lead you to say, "Sure, I grew up poor, but I want more for my family. I have plans." Or, "My skills as a parent are ones

I can use in the workplace. Organization, budgeting, and time management are all valuable in business." If you argue only *for your limitations*, you will keep them. I need you to start arguing *for your abilities*. Remember, whatever you focus on expands.

If you find yourself wandering off the path in front of you, it is in your control to get back on the right path—and *only you* can do that. No one else is going to take you by the hand and tug you back to where you should be. The best ways to get back on track are these:

- **Focusing on creating personal victories big or small:** No matter how tiny the victory is, celebrate it. Get addicted to the feeling of winning. Once you get a taste of it, you will never want to stop. If you are quitting smoking, celebrate going one hour without a cigarette, then two, then three. Each victory deserves a celebration, and I want you to be addicted to the things that empower you. If you do fall off the path for a moment, it will be easier to get back on it when you know what winning feels like.

- **Starving the negative thoughts:** I want you to starve those negative thoughts and anything else that is giving your energy to obstacles and excuses. Your power is always in the now. The faster you can starve negative thoughts in the now, the more victories you will have without falling into negative thoughts and actions.

    When you feel that opposing energy or opposing thought, stop yourself immediately. Reaffirm your

thoughts by revisiting the moment you said "Yes!" Get
back to feeling invincible as soon as you can. Remind
yourself why you are on this journey in the first place.
Talk yourself out of the negative space, and refocus
on your abilities and on that feeling you get when you
celebrate a victory. Your self-talk should be feeding
you life, not making you feel less than or regretful.

I have come across so many people who have chosen to participate in their own rescue. They have been people who have
come from nothing, who have faced every adversity, and who
had every reason to give up. The ones that made it big never gave
up on themselves. They stayed the course. They knew that no one
else could save them but themselves.

Anytime you find yourself wanting someone else to put more
energy into your own rescue, you are no longer the authority
of where you are headed. You have allowed yourself to become
the victim. Rescuing yourself requires all of your energy with
zero expectations of any outside support. Of course, help is always appreciated and welcomed, but it is much more beneficial
when you start with the old-adage mindset, "If it is to be, it's up
to me."

If it is your desire to master the millionaire mindset and become a first-generation millionaire, take personal control of your
final destination and be open for others to help you, but always
keep your hands on the wheel with full access to where you are
headed. Those who allow others to orchestrate their rescue will

always be subject to someone else's opinions, limitations, and direction.

A mentor of mine told me, "Johnny, never allow others to create your world for you because they will always create your world smaller than you can personally visualize for yourself." No one is qualified to see what you see for yourself.

My closest friend and mentor Holton Buggs, also a first-generation millionaire, is currently the wealthiest friend I have. He is a perfect example of someone who has participated in his or her own rescue. "Where I was growing up in Tampa," he told me, "I only hung around people who created a lid for me. I thought I could only go so far, because I wasn't exposed to anything else. I had thought I was exposed to a lot as a kid and in high school, but when I left home for the first time, I knew what I knew was nothing compared to what I could have."

But even as a child, he knew that he was around people who were not even trying to participate in their own rescue. His entire childhood was spent watching people who were waiting for someone to come along and rescue them. No one wanted more than what they had. No one wanted to escape the cycle they were in. It was not because they went out and looked around and decided not to try. It was because they didn't even go out and look around.

Luckily for him, his father's family owned a grocery store. When he was a kid, he would go to the wholesalers with his dad and buy food that he would resell to the kids at school. He went from selling popcorn bags for 25 cents a bag at recess to selling enough candy to buy a bike. Once he got a taste of entrepreneurship, he started cutting hair at his father's store for $4 a cut, and he earned enough to buy a car. He didn't know it at the time, but Holton was participating in his own rescue.

He took this mentality with him when he left home, and he built on it over and over again. Holton went on to make billions (no, that's not a typo) in revenue in network marketing, and he has recently opened his own company. He had to unlearn decades of watching his family members reach out a hand and take what was given instead of going out, making a commitment to a job or career, and working for their own success. It wasn't always easy, but he did it. He made this new way of looking at the world his.

We all are going to face curve balls in life. After all, life is a game. And right now, I am officially giving you permission to play the game to **win**.

I do want to acknowledge the reality that life happens to us all, and we will talk about mastering the art of response to unforeseen events later in the book. But, for now, I want you to master the art of staying in the driver's seat on your way to where you desire to be.

Anything that gets between you and your destiny is a temporary situation. It is not permanent. Be very careful to never allow a temporary moment to take up permanent mental residency. Allowing a difficult moment to become permanent will cause you to become bitter, and becoming bitter will be a catastrophic distraction to your personal breakthroughs. Mastering the art of the millionaire mindset is mastering the ability to become better, not bitter. Bitterness is the enemy because it leads to personal destruction.

Let me give you another example of how refusing to allow bitterness to live rent free in your brain will help clear your path. Fast-forwarding to my early thirties and no longer in the insurance industry but instead building entrepreneurs in the home-based business arena: I once mentored a young man from Brooklyn. After I spoke in Manhattan one night, he was chosen to drive me from the convention hall to Newark Airport. He hadn't had any success yet, but he had the unique ability to be coached in the moment. My leadership team knew that if we had some one-on-one time together, he would flourish. As we talked, I could tell he was driven but holding on to his past failures, and it was making him bitter. He was bitter at himself, his family, his partners, and his friends for doubting him. "I have done more than 400 presentations, and all of the people who heard my pitches said no. I just don't know what I am doing wrong!"

I told the young man, who was 10 years younger than I was, that we could spend the rest of the drive talking about the nos, but I'd rather talk about the yeses. I tried to explain to him that if he focused only on the obstacles, he would end up creating more obstacles. I wanted him to stop trying to fix what he was doing incorrectly and start replicating what was actually working. Take what was working, I said, and do it 30 times faster, 30 times stronger, and 30 times more frequently. It took me some time to get through to him, but he finally saw the light. He stopped being a whiner and focused only on the winning parts of his life. He stopped complaining and started participating in his own rescue.

When I met this young man in 2011, he was living paycheck to paycheck in the cramped Brooklyn apartment he shared with his fiancée and business partner along with their baby girl. Today, married with three kids. They left Brooklyn and now live in a beautiful, guarded, gated community in southern Florida. In the time that has passed since that long drive to Newark Airport, they have developed a global distribution team with a sales revenue that has exceeded $100 million. With a luxury sports car in the garage and all the amenities they need, he and his family now travel the world speaking to audiences, teaching others about how they became first-generation millionaires. I completely credit this to his ability to become better instead of being bitter.

———

I want you to come back to the idea of participating in your own rescue. Here is your first of many hard lessons to become a first-generation millionaire. Did you skip the introduction? If yes, why? What inside of you gives yourself permission to cut corners? If you skipped it, please do *not* allow yourself to move forward.

Learning to flex your first-generation-millionaire muscles "in the now" by correcting yourself, adapting, and refusing to cut corners will create a "**right-now**" mindset. If you have already started to cut corners, you are already straying off your path.

You *must* commit to my complete process 100 percent if you ever desire to break the generational mindsets that keep so many content with a life that is beneath their possibilities. I want you to be on the constant hunt for a life of fulfillment, not contentment. This was my first commitment to myself when I was still broke, living with a poverty mindset: "Johnny, no cutting corners!" Now go back and read the foreword, introduction, and the dedication. Trust me, you will be glad you did. I am very serious! If you did not read the introduction, stop now and go back and read it. If you decide to continue without reading the introduction, I promise you, you are a "corner cutter," and you most likely come from a long line of generational "corner cutters." How much longer do you want that to duplicate in your bloodline? All I am asking is that you make a commitment. Trust me, you will be glad you did.

What is your goal? Why did you buy this book? What made you start this journey? Whatever it is, focus on a winning mindset. What are the things that are working? How have you already moved your goal forward? What positive steps have you taken? Spend your time, energy, and resources thinking about these parts of your life and not what went wrong, where you failed, and the mistakes you have made. Harping on the negative is not the mindset of a winner. Remember, whiners never become first-generation millionaires. **Recognize your value** and exercise that muscle. It is time to build the character you need to achieve and sustain wealth. Start this important journey on the right foot.

ACTION STEP

Focus on something you have done that was successful. If you made ten calls and *one* was a success—*one* led to something successful—that's where you want to spend your time. Focus on what you did right, and multiply it. Just do it faster, stronger, and harder. Whiners will focus on what they did wrong and try to fix it. Winners will focus on what they did right and do it again and again and again.

Focus on where you were successful. Don't worry about where you were wrong. Worry about where you were right.

PILLAR 1

PARTICIPATING IN YOUR OWN RESCUE
FOCUS ON THE WIN

Today you're going to make sure you're a **winner** and not a whiner. The first step is to create a **winning mindset**.

The key to a winning mindset is focusing on your **successes**.

Your Assignment

What was the last goal you accomplished?
Write it here:

_____

_____

_____

_____

_____

_____

Now, three to five times today, think about and focus on that goal you achieved.

Embrace that **win**. Enjoy that **success**.

Most importantly, believe it's par for the course.

Now take a picture with the book and your filled-in answers and tag me on Instagram and Twitter (@wimbrey), as well as Facebook and LinkedIn. Share your progress and cheer on others!

Be sure to add our hashtags:

#BAMM

#WIMBREY

#CoachJohnny

Finding a Mentor

A huge part of my secret to success is that I constantly surround myself with thinkers who outthink me. I surround myself with the people who represent where I *want to be* in life. Without question, most of my success is due to the fact that I have **mentors**. You *must* have a mentor; you *must* submit yourself to thinking that is higher than your own. Without a mentor, you will never have the mindset of a winner. You will never achieve millionaire status. Unless you surround yourself with successful people, you can never truly rise to success.

Winners know what mentors can bring to them; whiners don't appreciate that value. As my favorite book—the Bible—says, "In the multitude of counsel, there is safety." If you don't have mentors—if you don't have counsel, if you don't have people speaking into your life—you can never be safe. It's that simple. Starting this very second, I want you to focus your efforts on creating the lifestyle of someone who desires and understands the importance of having mentors.

If you only submit to your own thinking, your own way of doing things, and your own worldview, then you will never grow as a person, and you will never be a first-generation millionaire. Having a mentor is absolutely crucial. The question is, how do you choose one?

Remember, you pick the mentor. Your mentor doesn't choose you. You don't have the luxury of waiting around for someone to notice you and take you under his or her wing. **You must participate in your own rescue.** In order to find the right mentor, you have to find someone who *already has what you value*. Seek out someone who already has the life that you want. Then you need to get access to that person, to that way of thinking, to that lifestyle.

I don't follow people who just sound good. I don't want a mentor who looks good on paper. I only look up to people who have proven success. When I was starting out pursuing a path in professional public speaking, I wanted someone who I thought was the best on the planet. I went straight to the top. For me, it was the number one motivational speaker, Les Brown. Let me be very clear: Les Brown didn't choose me. I chose Les Brown. I invested extreme amounts of time and money that I did not have because I knew if I got close to his voice, I would win. No one told me this; no one had to. I only had to hear him speak once to come to this crucial decision.

I heard Les Brown speak when I was in my early twenties, and I immediately knew he was the real deal. I had the extreme pleasure and honor of meeting Les Brown for the first time when I was 26 years old. For two years, I called him constantly, asking for advice, asking to meet, asking if there was anything I could do to help him whenever he was in town—carry his bag, drive him to the airport, *anything*. I was relentless. Finally, after two years of nonstop emails, he told me that he was coming to speak in Dallas-Fort Worth, my hometown, and that I was welcome to visit him in his hotel room before he went onstage. I was beside myself when I got that call. Les Brown's hotel room? Me? One-on-one time with the man I'd chosen as my mentor? This was it. This was going to be the beginning of a relationship I had wanted for years. I put on my best suit and headed over.

I opened the door to his suite and was shocked to find a huge group of people already there. I realized that this wasn't going to be the fireside chat I had envisioned on my way over, but I was still there. Even though I was just another person competing desperately for his attention, I was still doing so *in* Les Brown's hotel room. I was still honored to be there and soak it all in.

Finally, Les came over to me and started asking me questions: "How serious are you?"

I gave him everything I had: "Very serious. Very passionate. I went from being a teenager with a felony arrest to one of the top insurance sales reps in the country in less than five years. I have an incredible story, and I want to tell it right away. I want to tell it to as many people as I can."

"How would you like to be onstage with me tonight?" That question took my breath away. An opportunity like that would change my life. The exposure, the proximity to all these amazing speakers—it was the chance of a lifetime. He didn't even wait for me to answer. He knew I wanted it. "My buy-in is $20,000, but if you can meet me tonight with $5,000, I will put you onstage." Now, I knew Les Brown didn't need my money. This was a test, a challenge. He wanted to see how serious I was. I looked him right in the eye and told him I would see him onstage that night. I left immediately. I didn't need to stand around and listen to him talk to other people. I had my assignment—my mission—and I needed to find $5,000 in the next few hours.

I got in my car and started praying to God to make this happen. I hated the idea of asking people for *anything*. I was 26 years old and had been supporting myself since I was 16. Even though I lived under my father's roof in high school, for over a decade, I had earned every dollar I had, even for my clothes and my lunch money. I took pride in never putting my hand out to anyone. But this was different. I knew I needed to put my vanity aside and pick up the phone and start asking. By doing that— by conquering my ego—I was participating in my own rescue. I knew I had to leave my comfort zone or I would be stuck where I was forever.

My first call was to my stepmother, Joyce. She knew me better than just about anyone. It is very important for me that you understand that this was the absolute hardest phone call that I had ever made in my adult life up to that point. Why? Because I had never asked anyone in my family for anything as an adult, and that was my personal trophy to myself. Making this phone call would be me destroying my personal trophy of "self-accomplishment," but I knew that a far greater trophy would present itself and would ultimately set me on a new trajectory in life as one of the greatest motivational speakers of my time and possibly one of the best to ever live. She knew that if I was asking her for something, that something was incredibly important to me. I told her about this opportunity. I told her it would change my life forever. I told her I needed $5,000.

Her exact words to me were, "Where are you now?"

I told her I was driving south through Dallas, headed back to my home in South Dallas. She told me to meet her at the hospital where she worked so she could give me half of it. I started crying. One phone call, and I had half the money. My prayers were being answered.

As I drove to the hospital, my friend Tony Hobbs called me. I had known Tony for years. We grew up on the streets together, and we had done what no teenagers should do to make money. He knew who I had been before and who I was becoming now. I loved Tony, but I knew that I had to get him off of the phone and start my other calls before it was too late. "Tony. I want to talk, but let me hit you back. I have the chance to speak on the same stage as Les Brown tonight, but I need $2,500 to get up there."

"Wait," he said. "Les Brown? The speaker?" Now I was floored. How did *Tony* know who *Les Brown* was? I asked him as much. "He came and spoke at my church the other day. He is the real deal."

"Wow, that's great, man, but I still need to call you back later. I need to go find this money."

Tony's exact words: "Johnny. Where are you?" I said I was headed south on loop 12 passing the Potters House Church about to make a quick stop in Arlington to pick up the first half from my stepmother. Tony's next words were, "Can you meet me at the gas station that is on the way? I got the other half in cash on me right now."

As soon as the words came out of his mouth, I was in tears. Honestly, I was so emotional I probably should not have been driving, but nothing was going to stop me now. I was in the midst of my destiny. When I saw Tony 10 minutes later, he put $2,500 cash in my hand. Just like that. I was in.

That night indeed changed my life. Les became my mentor and a huge part of who I am and who I wanted to be as a speaker and a businessman. In less than five minutes, I had made one call and then taken another call that came to me, and suddenly that incredible chance of sharing the stage with the world's number one motivational speaker was mine to take. If I had let my pride get in the way, there is no way I would have found the money I needed. There is no way I would have become what I am today. **I participated in my own rescue and found a mentor who was where I wanted to be and who wanted to see me reach my goals. Not only did I participate in my own rescue, but I also invested time, swallowed my pride, and humbled myself in order to do it.**

It's OK to look at other people and want their lifestyle. It's OK to want what they have. It's OK to watch what they are doing and emulate them. It's okay to ultimately surpass them. A true mentor will be happy for you when you do. All good mentors have an equal desire to see you succeed. Choose someone who won't put you down, rub your failures in your face, or make you feel less than your true value.

Finding your own mentor doesn't have to be an insurmountable step. Anyone can be your mentor. You don't have to go looking for the titan of industry, a published author, or someone on television or the radio. It can be an esteemed coworker, a friend you look up to, a teacher you trust, or even an older family member.

No matter where you find your mentors, they should have the following qualities:

1. They have a lifestyle you desire and respect.

2. They have a genuine desire to see you win.

3. They are supportive of your surpassing them in business and at potentially no longer needing their mentorship.

4. They are firm, yet fair and friendly.

Once you have decided that you would like someone to be your mentor, you will need to actually ask that person if he or she would be willing to dedicate his or her time, knowledge, and energy to helping you grow. Here are a few ways to approach a possible mentor for current or for future possibilities:

1. **Offer to serve and volunteer in any capacity possible.** When you do this, be sure your eyes and ears are at full attention 100 percent of the time. And only speak when spoken to. (Examples of how you can serve include airport pickups, carrying the luggage, and providing personal security if needed.) By volunteering and articulating your reasons for wanting to be close and soak up as much wisdom as possible, you will show transparency, which leads to trust. You'll be amazed by how far volunteering can get you. And when the right door opens, it's because there is something about *you* that your mentor likes.

2. **Find a way to become beneficial to the mentor's mission.** Offer your personal expertise without compensation or motive. A true mentor will know your motive, so there is no need to explain unless asked.

3. **Let the mentor know how much his or her work has affected your life.** With confidence and transparency, let the mentor know you want to be an ambassador of the mentor's cause or mission because of how that work has affected you personally. Know the mentor's works, publications, accomplishments, and achievements.

4. **Anticipate the mentor's needs.** Your mentor's inner circle will open up based on your ability to know what the mentor needs or wants before the mentor asks. When my mentors licked their lips or coughed, I would approach with water, a cough drop, or a tissue. I was already prepared. I didn't wait to be asked for things. Be ready all the time when you are near your mentor; you never know when it will be your time to step up. Stay ready, so you never have to get ready.

If the mentor you want to work with says he or she can't take on a mentee right now, that's OK. You can always set yourself up for a future possibility. Let the mentor know that regardless of time, distance, or convenience, the mentor should add you to the top of his or her list the next time the mentor needs any service. Make a verbal confession that you have a burning desire to be close to greatness. For example, you could say: "My desire is to *not* be seen or heard. My desire is to serve so as to be close to your wisdom."

And remember, you don't always need to be in personal contact to have a mentor. You can also get what you need from your mentor even if you never meet in person. You can be mentored from afar, by reading what the mentor writes, subscribing to the mentor's newsletters, podcasts, and shows, and attending the mentor's speaking engagements.

While my friend Holton Buggs was in college at Texas Southern University in Houston, he started working in network marketing to make some money on the side. At one of the first seminars Holton attended, the main speaker was Bill Britt, a man who had earned billions in the industry. It was then and there that Holton decided that this was the man he was going to follow in order to find the success he wanted so much.

Yet, in all the years he has followed Bill Britt, Holton has never actually *met* him or even shaken his hand. But what he has done is listen to every word Bill has said publicly. And he followed every piece of advice he heard. In the end, Holton realized that he didn't need to meet Bill in person. He just needed to follow and adopt Bill's philosophy. Bill never knew who Holton was, but Bill still mentored him. And as a result, he changed Holton's life because Holton started to have more confidence and to speak in terms of goals.

Winners understand and realize that they need someone in their court, someone who will be a role model and an advisor. Whiners do not. A whiner says, "I am my own person. I don't need anyone to tell me what to do. I can do this by myself." Those words may sound like strength, but they actually come from someone who is too weak to reach out and ask others for guidance and help. Don't be that person.

Just as Holton and I have done, look outside your bubble, and discover things that you never even knew you wanted. If you think there is only *one* way to become a first-generation millionaire, you will fail. Be open to other possibilities, other paths, and other points of view. A mentor will be your guide on this journey. Find one you trust before you walk too far down this path. You want to find a mentor who has every desire for you to pass him or her. A true mentor will never hold you down and will never be intimidated by your rise to success.

I used to be someone who tried to do it all on my own. When I wrote my first book, I wanted complete ownership. And I had it. I spent tens of thousands of dollars on printers and distribution and storage. I had to learn how to navigate the publishing world on my own. I had to take responsibility for the decision to write and publish my book. I don't regret it, but I also know that resisting that lone-ranger mindset and thinking outside the box would have done me a world of good. What if I had reached out to some authors to ask them for advice? What if I had tried to work with a publisher instead of striking out on my own? The book went on to become my bestselling book—I printed over 250,000 copies, and it has been read around the world—but I still tucked those lessons away for the future.

Now, I can pass those lessons on to my mentees. Instead of encouraging each of them to write a book and navigate the same hurdles I experienced, I have worked out a system that allows them to write a chapter in a book that I spearhead, market, and publish. Ten up-and-coming speakers and entrepreneurs write one chapter each, all contributing to an impressive, jaw-dropping book that they can use to make connections, build their brand, and sell on their own. They don't have to spend their own money, time, and resources to write and publish a book they can be proud of.

When these writers open themselves up to my mentorship, they are getting my decades of experiences, my guidance, and the lessons of my past. I want more for them than what I have, and showing them an easier way to succeed makes me a good mentor.

Look for this type of selflessness, benevolence, and empathy in your own mentor. You don't want someone who wants to punish you, to make sure you pay your dues and go through everything the mentor went through on his or her way up. The whole idea of having a mentor is to avoid pitfalls and skip the mistakes that take up too much of your time and energy.

Showing you the right path and making sure you learn from their mistakes should be the mission of all mentors. They should want to accelerate you while keeping you safe. You want mentors who will gift you with their experience and show you the best way forward. Once you find those mentors, build those relationships from the ground up. They will help you for the rest of your life.

Finding a mentor comes down to commitment. **Do you have the tenacity and commitment to find someone you deserve?** I never said this was going to be easy. Not everyone has the stomach to leave their comfort zone. If this is not you, then give this book to someone else. But if it is you, go all in. This is a hard journey, and you need someone in your court who has been there before. Choose someone, and then put in that *whole dollar* exactly as we discussed in the introduction. You will be pleasantly surprised by your return on that investment. Holton did this with Bill Britt, and it had an enormous impact on his life.

ACTION STEP

Get on social media and find someone—local or international, man or woman, in your field or not—whom you want to have access to. Read everything that person has written. Listen to every podcast. Watch every video. And then, even though all of that could be enough, I want you to take it to the next level.

Once you know that this is the person for you—and here is the hardest part—reach out to him or her. Email that person. Message him or her on social media. Call and leave messages. Stop by that person's offices if you can. The absolute most respectful and beneficial way is to offer any value or services that you can bring to that person instantly. Offer to be an airport shuttle. Offer to carry his or her bags, and be willing to serve in any capacity just to be in his or her presence.

I would *never* have gotten access to Les Brown if I hadn't kicked the door open. I am giving you permission to beat on some doors. Find 10 people whose lifestyles you desire. Get in touch with the top 3. Then get in touch with the next 3. Keep going. **Participate in your own rescue.**

A whiner will ask, "What if they ignore me? What if I can't get access to them? What if I embarrass myself?" A winner will ask, "What if I *can*? What if they answer me? What if it *does* work?" Be a winner. Participate in your own rescue, and choose mentors who will get you to where you want to be in life.

PILLAR 2

FINDING A MENTOR

BECOME A PROFESSIONAL STALKER

Success is **contagious**.

Start surrounding yourself with people who have already achieved the things you want, and I guarantee you'll reach your goals **10 times faster**.

I want you to get **closer** to people who have what you desire.

Your Assignment

Using social media, find **10 people** who are doing what you're doing. Follow them. Become a professional stalker.

Then, **contact** and **connect with them**. Mark the date in the Connected column only *after* you're in touch.

	Name	Date Connected
1.		
2.		
3.		
4.		
5.		
6.		
7.		
8.		
9.		
10.		

Now take a picture with the book and your filled-in answers, and tag me on Instagram and Twitter (@wimbrey), as well as on Facebook and LinkedIn (feel free to black out the names if you want to keep them private). Share your progress and cheer on others!

Be sure to add our hashtags:

#BAMM

#WIMBREY

#CoachJohnny

Establishing Accountability

Y ou have your goal in front of you: becoming a first-generation millionaire. You have started the search for a mentor. You believe in your value, you have faith in yourself, and you are committed to your cause. Now what? You need **accountability**. It is well and good to have all these pieces ready to go, but you must have a driving factor in your life that will keep you moving forward. This is where accountability comes in. While your mentor can hold you accountable, that is not his or her primary job. You need to find someone who cares about you, who is invested in your success, and who will help you stay on track. I had such a person in my own life when I was working on one of my first big projects.

In my church leadership program, I was blessed to be surrounded by truly special, genuine people every week. One of my fellow students at the time, Christopher Lloyd (no, not the actor), is such a person. When he asks you how you are, he is not just making conversation. He truly cares about how your day is going. It is a rare gift that everyone around him appreciates, and it was especially appreciated during that grueling leadership training.

This was back in 2002. I was 27 years old. Christopher and I were both high-level students in an exclusive leadership class that required major service and volunteering. I served so much back then that I had holes in my shoes, but I could not afford to replace them. My oldest daughter had been born the year before, and my wife was pregnant with our second. It was an extremely tough time for all of us. But I served through pain and tears because I was so hungry to learn leadership. And a major part of learning was getting through endless days of serving leaders by driving and being on hotel duty and acting as their security detail. While it meant long days and time away from my family, it was this service that got me in the presence of very influential global trailblazers. I was not allowed to talk to or engage with them unless they started a conversation with me first, but that didn't matter because I had always found that the best way to learn was to watch, not talk. Christopher and I did this for years, bringing us closer and building our character together.

When I was writing my first book—*From the Hood to Doing Good*—I needed to describe it to everyone I knew in order to make it real, to make it happen. If I had kept talking about the book, but no book appeared, everyone would know that I hadn't followed through on my goals. I knew if I told Christopher, he would ask me about how the book was going every time he saw me—at least twice a week in our leadership meetings. And he did. Every time he asked, I would reply, "Fine." As long as I thought about the book, wrote some notes down, or even talked about it, I would reply, "Fine." But in truth, nothing was happening. Months went by, and all I was doing was spinning my wheels. Christopher's questions only reminded me that I was not getting anywhere on a project that was very important to me. I was going from being a winner to being a whiner.

One day, before Christopher could ask me how the book was going, I cut him off. "Enough of asking me how it's going. From now on, I want you to ask what page I am on." I knew that if I had to see him twice a week, I wouldn't be able to stand repeating the same page number even once. I would be extremely embarrassed about my lack of progress, especially when I had to say it out loud. "Fine" was no longer going to cut it. Christopher was holding me accountable, even if *he* didn't know it.

After that, I finished the book within a month, proudly giving Christopher a new number every time he asked me what page I was on. My plan worked only because I knew Christopher cared so much, that he had a genuine interest in my success, and that he was paying attention. I would have never trusted my accountability to someone who only half listened, or forgot to ask me, or didn't even remember I was writing a book. My accountability was precious to me.

Be very careful to never place your precious jewels into the mouths of pigs. As it is written in ancient writings, "Do not cast your pearls amongst swine." I was not about to cast my pearls among swine. A pig will eat a million dollars in cash! Why? Swine have no concept of value or extravagance. Likewise, never cast your ideas or goals onto the ears of someone who has no interest in seeing you succeed. The faster you learn the value of protecting your ideas, visions, or intellectual property, the more likely you are to establish a millionaire mindset. Why? When you decrease the invitations and opportunities for negative noise and distractions, you become more empowered with divine discernment of whom to allow into your inner circle for support and accountability. Only those who have a genuine interest in my success have access to anything that's building my future wealth. The danger of allowing random people into your **success circle** just to impress them could be a self-inflicted death blow killing your ability to truly establish a millionaire mindset.

I established accountability without permission. Most people wouldn't have known the difference between asking me about my book or asking me about the weather. It was all the same to them. Instead, I chose someone special, someone who cared about me, someone who took a keen interest in me and my life, and someone who would hold me accountable. **I knew that by doing so, I was pushing myself forward and participating in my own rescue.**

My experience with accountability goes both ways. For every time I have asked someone to keep me accountable, I have done the same for someone else. Take my amazing mentee Lillie Ennis from Connecticut as an example. Very soon after she started working with me, she began scaling the ladder quickly and aggressively, landing a very significant rank in the company right out of the gate. I was very impressed, but I didn't want her to rest on her laurels. It was wonderful, what she had accomplished, but I knew she had more in her.

I told her, "If lightning strikes once, that's great. But it is really special when lightning strikes twice. I want lightning to strike you twice." I told her to take what she did in her own accounts and duplicate that success with someone on her team. She said to me later, "When you told me this, it was my first time meeting you, and honestly, I was surprised. Any other boss or mentor would have blown smoke up my ass, would have told me that I was doing a great job, and to just keep doing well. But not you. You said, 'You did well. Now you can do better.' I took this push and made sure you held me accountable to the task."

Lillie chose a member of her team and mentored him with the same lessons I had taught her. He excelled, and her rank in the company grew even higher. "I would have never hit that next level if Johnny hadn't given me that accountability. Instead of saying 'You are doing great,' Johnny always gave me a challenge. He is good at giving you homework. He never settles and never wants his mentees to settle either."

Finding someone or something (like an app or tracking system) that will hold you accountable speaks directly to your commitment. Share that commitment with someone else if you can. Remember, the vending machine will not give you half a bag. Getting someone to hold you accountable is part of putting that whole dollar in and getting the whole bag out. You won't succeed in becoming a first-generation millionaire if you don't put in that whole dollar.

The first step in getting an accountability partner is to find the right person. Do this by looking for people with the following qualities:

1. They have a genuine interest in you. They genuinely desire to see you win. They have no personal motives or expectations to benefit other than being proud of you.

2. They are already inquisitive and excited to listen when you talk. Invite them into your goals without making it sound like homework. Make it effortless—no one wants helping you to be their part-time job. An easy assignment can be established by simply sharing a current project with them and asking them to hold you accountable on completion.

3. They are not full of fluff and just stroking your ego. They actually challenge you in conversation in a way that encourages you to become better.

Then, make sure you put yourself in a position to see or hear from them regularly, establish frequent accountability, and be extremely transparent with your progress and failures. This will ensure that you are not going to back down. Here are two possible scripts you can use to start the accountability process:

Script 1

"Hey, Chris, how are you?"

"Doing good, Johnny. Just staying busy."

"I hear you, man. I'm staying busy myself getting back into shape physically."

"Really, what are you doing to make that possible?"

"Nothing major, just daily activities that increase my heart rate to burn calories. As a matter of fact, Chris, do me a favor please. Every time you see me or we talk, ask me how many minutes of cardio I did the day before."

Script 2

"Hey guys, I am trying to push myself a little with my sales goals this week."

"Oh, yeah? What did you have in mind?"

"Well, how about we each share our numbers at the end of every day, no matter how high or low. Seeing how we all are doing will be a great kick in the pants to get me over this line."

I used Script 2 when I was first starting out and wanted to be the first one to reach the highest level in my rank in global sales. Not only did I reach my goal but all my buddies leveled up too. It was the perfect way to keep us all accountable.

Adapt these scripts to your situation and personality—and keep them simple! After starting the process of finding mentors, you are responsible for putting yourself in a position for them to ask the question, whether that's in person, via social media, or by phone. Be extremely honest (this is your life), and show your gratitude that they asked, and tell them that their question has held you accountable and it is working. This will show you how far you have come. If these mentors are a good fit for you, keep going. If they aren't, then find others who are.

Speaking of a good fit, it's important that you find the people or resources that fit your personality type. An application or online tracker that shows you your daily progress might be the best fit for you because you don't need someone else holding you accountable if you can see your progress (or lack thereof) on a screen. But others might be more successful working with people, as opposed to online trackers, because they will feel more embarrassment if they don't succeed. What works for me might not work for you, and what works for you may not be a good fit for me. That's fine. As long as you find something that works, that's all that matters!

ACTION STEP

Ask yourself: What is my goal? Why am I here? Why did I pick up this book? What do I want from this? Once you have that figured out, *tell someone else who has a genuine desire to see you win in life.* Don't just tell him or her what you are doing, however. Make sure you share where you are in the process.

Accountability isn't just saying everything is good and moving on. I want you to create a lifestyle of a winner. Team up with people who want to see you succeed. Choose people who have a desire to see you be a winner in your life. Chris was excited for me, but he didn't have a tangible way to help me. When I changed his question from "How is it going?" to "What page are you on?" I gave him that power. The fact that he was asking me "What page?" put me at risk of being embarrassed. That risk of embarrassment pushed me to keep going and ultimately finish my book within a month.

If I can do it, you can do it. Never be afraid to throw yourself into the deep end. There are generations depending on you. You cannot learn how to swim in shallow water. Establishing accountability is throwing yourself into the deep water, and that's where you will find your first-generation-millionaire mindset.

Write out your vision, and make it extremely clear: a certain number of calls a day, or more money in your account, or a list of dream partnerships you want to make. Invite someone into that vision who has a genuine desire to see you win. Make that person a part of your goal. It may be awkward. It may be uncomfortable. But you will never learn to swim in shallow water. It may be scary at first, but you won't progress if you are hanging on to that pool wall. Go find that accountability partner. Write the vision. Invite him or her into that vision. Participate in your rescue. Commit to your goal. If you cannot do these things, then you will never rise to first-generation-millionaire status.

PILLAR 3

ESTABLISHING ACCOUNTABILITY
CHOOSE YOUR PARTNER

External accountability will transform your productivity. The key is finding people who are **invested** in your success—and who will also ask you the hard questions.

Your Assignment

Find people who **celebrate** you, not tolerate you. Tell them your **goal**. Then ask them to help you track your progress.

This requires a **benchmark**. They need to know where you are on your path toward your goal.

For example, if your goal is to increase your weekly income, your accountability partners should know your current income. Then, a week later, they should ask, "How much did you make this week?"

Name an accountability partner below, and when he or she has accepted the responsibility, mark it as accepted:

My **goal** is: _____

My **accountability partner** is: _____

He or she accepted on: _____

Now take a picture with the book and your filled-in answers, and tag me on Instagram and Twitter (@wimbrey),

as well as on Facebook and LinkedIn. Share your progress and cheer on others!

Be sure to add our hashtags:

#BAMM

#WIMBREY

#CoachJohnny

PART I
PREPARATION VERSUS IMPROVISATION

I f you want to master this thing called wealth, you have to become a master of **preparation**. People who prepare have a vision and a goal. They prepare for every win and loss on the horizon. People who improvise are led by the wind. They may be talented and gifted in business, but they can also be their own worst enemy. Every day could mean a new idea or a new vision, but those ideas will never be realized if they are simply blown around. My mentor Les Brown taught me a principle that I have used for years and that I will pass on to my children: "It is better to be prepared and not called than to be called and not prepared."

Let me be very clear: wanting **the call** for success does not make you unique. Everyone wants the call. What makes you unique is preparing for the call and never knowing when or if it's going to come. Preparation is a millionaire mindset. Making *the when*, *the how*, and *the where* none of your business but refusing to get out of position is a masterful level of the millionaire mindset. I want you to master the art of being prepared. I want you to commit to a mindset of preparation. Without that commitment, you will never be able to break the cycle of *generational existence*. Existing alone is not enough to create a legacy of generational wealth.

Setting Your Goals

The first step to being prepared is setting your goals in a way that allows you to follow through with them. Don't say, "I want to change my industry and make money doing so." Instead, set concrete and specific goals that you can envision yourself meeting on a daily basis. "I want to partner with these three people." "I want to open an office and hire a staff." "I want to get my product and ideas on this particular platform." Ideas and goals are amazing things, but without follow-through, you will just become an improviser with nothing to show for your ideas at the end of the day.

My good friend Larry Brown, whom I love as a brother, is a perfect example of a (former) improviser. I want you to understand the magnitude of this example I am about to lay out. As I write this, *only* 47 people in the history of the National Football

League have earned the title Super Bowl MVP. Larry is a three-time Super Bowl champion with the Dallas Cowboys. He's a very good friend of mine, and he was constantly coming up with a brilliant new idea.

Back in 2001, after appearing on Dave Letterman's and Jay Leno's talk shows, Larry wanted to transition from being a ball player to being a businessman. We met in church, and he started mentoring me soon after. He was the first celebrity I was close to, and spending time with him and getting a taste of his lifestyle was an eye-opener. I was in my early twenties and not yet married, and as I spent more time with Larry, I learned more and more about what I could do if I found success. It only drove me harder.

I had been hanging out with Larry for a while when my friend Pete Vargas called me. He was still in college, working as a youth minister, and he wanted me to ask Larry if he would come and speak to his kids. Larry was happy to, but only on the condition that I would be invited (and paid) as well. That was just who Larry was (and is to this day).

On the day of the event, Larry and I got in this tiny plane to go speak to this youth group in Hereford, Texas, a town that is known for its cattle and beef industry. During the 30-minute flight, he began selling me on the idea of bringing the video game world to the internet. Now, Larry is a very high level visionary, and this idea was way ahead of his time. As he spoke, I became more and more excited, and I told him that we *had* to make this happen as soon as we got back. The idea was a money-maker; I knew it. What I didn't know at the time was that even though Larry was an amazing visionary, he didn't have a plan in place. Larry talked about his ideas as if they were in their final stages, but in fact, this amazing idea was something he had just come up with.

When we landed in Hereford, everyone was so excited to meet the amazing Larry Brown—the kids, the parents, everyone. Billionaires in the cattle industry were lining up to shake his hand. It was an amazing event, and we both got a fantastic amount of exposure. I was riding high from Larry's gaming idea and the event, but when we got back to the hotel, Larry sat me down to talk about another idea he had.

The same man from the plane now had a new passionate idea about cattle. He spoke to me as if it were the only idea he had ever had. I was floored. What happened to the gaming idea? What was going to happen to this idea when he had another epiphany? In that moment, I realized that while Larry was clearly brilliant, he wasn't going to do anything big if he didn't put his ideas into practice.

Larry was a master of vision, but he didn't have a team around him or even a plan of attack to make those visions happen. When he played ball, his team would protect him from what he didn't see and tell him when things were not going to work out. Larry had to learn how to create a team around him. Remember, in the multitude of counsel is safety. This statement applies to your support team and plan as well as to your mentors.

In the end, both ideas became wasted opportunities. Someone else took on the video game industry and the internet, and someone else revolutionized the beef industry. Happily, Larry is not that guy anymore though. He is now a successful professional speaker, television sports personality, and investor with a clear vision of what he wants for his future. I want you to learn from him. I want you to see what mistakes he made, so that you never make the same ones.

You don't need to be like Larry. You don't have to be an idea machine. Amazing things can happen when you take just *one* idea and put all your effort behind it. When you have your big idea or your big goal, when you're ready to make the investment in yourself and follow through, attack that plan with passion. You will enjoy your rise so much more if you connect your endeavors to something you love. By making a choice about what you want and deciding to start working toward it, you are **participating in your own rescue**.

Goals are tricky things. Ever since we were in grade school, we have been taught to set huge, long-term goals. "What do you want to be when you grow up?" "A fireman! A doctor! President!" Now, those of us who have kids—hell, those of us who *were* kids!—know that these big goals can change. They almost always do.

Setting goals can be daunting. It's easy to think about things you want in the long term. You want to be a millionaire. You want to pay off your mortgage and buy a vacation house. You want to start your own business. You want to earn enough to take your family on vacation every few months. But if you don't break those big goals down into smaller ones that allow you to make progress each day toward that big goal, you will never be able to get what you want.

Think of a ladder. Your ultimate goal is that top rung or step, and you are currently at the bottom rung. You can't get from the bottom to the top without all those rungs in the middle. Setting huge, lofty goals may seem satisfying at first, but that feeling doesn't last long unless you have all the rungs planned out. Long-term goals are all well and good, but it is the short-term ones that will get you results that you can build upon.

Contrary to popular belief, setting a goal is not an indication that you are on your way to mastering the mindset of a first-generation millionaire. Not even close! Setting a goal is simply an indication that you have your eyes on the prize with the intent of accomplishment. Writing a goal is a personal declaration that you have a desire to **start**. Anyone can set a goal, but the sad reality is that most people who set a goal never start. Champions who truly have a burning desire to win don't just **set the goal**. They **get the goal.** I have heard many speakers and coaches train people in how to set the goal, and that's good, but those who train people in how to **get the goal** create the slight edge advantage of teaching people how to actually reach that goal. How do you go from being a goal setter to becoming a goal getter? The truth is, there are many ways to exercise this **mental muscle,** but what follows is one of the most proven, practical, and best step-by-step principles I have ever witnessed.

My mentor Holton Buggs was the first person I have ever heard teach a version of this concept years ago. Since then, I've taken his concept and transformed it into something that now works perfectly for me: the **90-Day Get-the-Goal Challenge.**

To start the challenge, I first want you to think of a ladder. Each rung, or step, is your measured progress toward your goal. Your goal ladder represents a short-term goal that you want to reach in the next 90 days. Right now, take out a piece of paper and draw a ladder with five rungs. Write down your big idea—your big goal—on the top rung. Now, write down one smaller, achievable goal that will help you get there on the bottom rung. You can sketch out the four other rungs if you want, but that isn't as important right now. That first rung is your first 90-day goal.

Next on your ladder (or on a separate piece of paper), break up that first goal into a halfway point. Use a pen, not a pencil. These are not sketches. They are set in stone for the next 90 days. Where do you need to be at that halfway point? Say you want to write that book or get a certain number of customers every single month. You can't just go from zero to finished book or 20 customers to 100 customers a month. You have to build up to it. If you want to write a 200-page book, then at the halfway point, you need to have 100 pages written. Now that you have your halfway point (45 days from your start), break that down into 15 days, 30 days, 60 days, and 75 days, and write those goals next to them.

If you want to talk to 60 potential customers every single day, then you know that by the 45-day mark, you will need to be talking to at least 30 people every single day. But know that those numbers won't happen right away. Build up to it. Start by mastering talking to 15 people every day. Then 20. Once you know you can hit those numbers consistently, move up to 30 people a day. If you reach half your goal, great, but use those benchmarks as guides.

Stay on track and watch those benchmarks. Focus on those smaller goals and not the goal at top of the ladder. While that top-rung goal is important, know that it may change over time, due to changing circumstances—a death in your family, a new baby, or even a global pandemic. Also keep in mind that if your top-rung goal is too big or too vague, you can get discouraged if you aren't seeing that goal happen right away.

Once you have reached that first rung, repeat this exercise for the next rung, and the rung after that. Add rungs to your ladder if you need to. And remember, it's OK to amend that top-rung goal as you see yourself scaling the ladder. It may get bigger. It may expand or adjust as you change industries or professions or as you discover things about yourself as you climb this ladder. All of that's OK. Focus on those smaller 90-day goals. They will lay the foundation for your success.

The amazing thing about implementing this principle in your life is that you can aim it at any goal (losing weight, increasing your savings accounts, increasing your annual income, quitting smoking). There are zero limitations. Here's why. Imagine a 90-dot connect-the-dots puzzle. It is more important to focus on the next dot that is already in sight than it is to focus on the end result. It's the same process when it comes to practicing your 90-Day Get-the-Goal Challenge. The more you practice this process in multiple areas in your life, the more this new strategy will become part of your lifestyle, which will ultimately lead you to becoming a master of the millionaire mindset.

———

I want you to be a visionary. I want you to think of great ideas. But I also want you to pick one good idea and prepare for it. Just give yourself one goal to focus on *right now* and *make it count*. Don't live in the land of improvisation. Don't improvise your life and continue to think you're on your way to becoming wealthy when you are not.

If you don't plan the rungs of your ladder, then you have no way of knowing if you are actually working toward what you want. You have no way of measuring your growth. You have no way of knowing if you are on the right track.

If you truly want to be a first-generation millionaire, if you truly want to master the art of wealth, then you have to put your goals into action. **Have faith in yourself and your ideas.** Pay attention to your ideas, and implement them. Be brilliant. Stay focused. Prepare. Hit your goal. If you aren't willing to do so, you have no business on this journey to becoming a first-generation millionaire.

ACTION STEP

I want you to start with your first goal and work backward. I want you to isolate that goal and trace backward to that exact number of what you need to do each week or day to reach your goal. Once you do it one day, then two days in a row, then three days, you will know what success feels like.

The evidence of hitting those goals every day and every week will build the commitment key of your character, making you a master of your wealth and success.

PILLAR 4

SETTING YOUR GOALS
PRIORITIZE AND SET BENCHMARKS

Not everyone has brilliant ideas—but even fewer follow through on the great ideas they do have. **Preparation** is the foundation of **execution**. If you want to accomplish your goals, you must first prioritize and set benchmarks.

Your Assignment

You're here, so I know you have a goal in mind. Now it's time to **focus**. Put your strongest idea at the top of your ladder, and sketch out the rungs. Then plan out that first rung, your first 90-day goal.

Put this breakdown in a place you see every day.

90-Day Goal

By Day 15, I will: _____

By Day 30, I will: _____

By Day 45, I will: _____

By Day 60, I will: _____

By Day 75, I will: _____

Accomplishing this task will provide a **plan of action** and ensure that you don't lose focus.

Weave the other two into the ladder, if you can. It's OK to move higher rungs around and swap them out as you reach each 90-day goal.

Now take a picture with the book and your filled-in answers, and tag me on Instagram and Twitter (@wimbrey), as well as on Facebook and LinkedIn. Share your progress and cheer on others!

Be sure to add our hashtags:

#BAMM

#WIMBREY

#CoachJohnny

Being Busy Versus Being Productive

The biggest lie ever told is this: busy means productive. The truth is that you could be working hard, staying up nights, getting up early, putting in the hours, and still be moving in the wrong direction. You can feel like you are doing all the right things when in fact, you are moving further away from your goal. It's an easy trap to fall into. I've done it. Countless other successful people have done it.

If you are taking care of others besides yourself, you know how busy things can get. But just being busy doesn't mean you are being productive. For example, some of us will go through the entire house to pick up three items of clothing and bring them to the laundry room. Instead, we can choose two days out of the week to focus on laundry. A lot of us are also on the look-out for a good bargain. We keep an eye on what's on sale at Walmart and know what days are best to hit Target. Because of this, we may go out one day for a gallon of milk and then make a completely separate trip on another day to another store to get a jar of peanut butter. Instead, we could pick one day out of the week to do all the food shopping rather than constantly making trips to the store. Making multiple trips is busy, for sure, but it's not productive. It is much more productive to have full days of activity when you know you are going to get everything on your list done in one fell swoop. In this pillar, I want you to internalize the difference between busy and productive.

None of us are perfect. We are all going to have to learn as we go. Right now, I want you to focus on the accomplishment, not the activity. Some people get satisfaction as a result of their intentions. They listen to online seminars for eight hours and proudly tell everyone that they worked on their business all day. They make list after list after list and call it a day. Those are not accomplishments. They are activities. Don't get lost in the activity, and don't let the satisfaction from a completed activity cloud your judgment. Instead of making to-do lists, focus on the list of what you actually did all day. List the accomplishments you have already completed, and focus on those.

Being too busy to be productive is like being on an airplane that is going in the wrong direction. Think about it. Even though it's one of the most amazing inventions ever—a massively productive force—it can do everything it is meant to do and still actually be unproductive. How? Its engines can be in tip-top shape and its pilot and staff can be top notch, but if it is going in the wrong direction, all that effort and energy and engineering is actually taking it away from its ultimate goal. Sure, it's doing what it was designed to do, but it is not actually getting you to where you need to be.

"What does this have to do with me, Johnny?" you might ask. Well. I've been in sales my entire life. At 18 and 19, I was a telemarketer while working my way through acting school. Then I became a licensed insurance agent and earned my license to sell home security systems for the state of Texas. Then I started my own business. I have sold books, companies, and partnerships. In all those years of salesmanship, here is what I have learned: just because people look busy, it doesn't mean that they are productive. I have seen so many people in the home-based business sector lose so much because they are *too busy* to actually be productive. They work and plan and work and plan, but they don't actually move the needle in the right direction. It's heartbreaking to watch.

Take the people who do sales blitzes as an example. A *blitz* typically means you are going to go all out, put all your effort into selling, selling, selling—for 1 day, for 7 days, even for 90 days. It sounds impressive, right? But here is the problem: just because people are busy being busy, it doesn't mean they are doing something productive. In sales, people think throwing things up against the wall to see what sticks is being productive. But it is not. You can't just pick up the phone and call everyone on your list. You need to make sure that you make each call in a way that brings you closer to your goal. You can't waste time trying everything to see if even half the things work. The things that don't work are a waste of your time. You must attack all of your calls and strategies as if you have an **emotional connection** to each and every one of those attempts.

I've seen people go into war rooms, just dialing and making calls, but they don't know *whom* they are calling or *why* they are calling them. What's the most effective way to reach out to this person? If you don't have the *who*, *why*, and *what* answered before you go in, you run the risk of being very busy but unproductive. Wayne Gretzky has said that "100 percent of the shots you don't take never go in." But Wayne didn't take his hockey stick to the baseball field hoping to hit a home run. He didn't take it to the golf course thinking he would win the Stanley Cup. He focused his attention and energy on hockey and succeeded.

I want you to swing, I want you to be aggressive, I want you to charge toward your passion—as long as what you are charging toward is actually part of your target.

Value your time. Value your experience. And value your education. So many of my mentees have invested so much in themselves—through seminars, through classes, and through simply doing the work. When they start to rise, however, friends and acquaintances flock to them for free advice. They then become busy helping others for free, which is the opposite of productivity. I tell them that in order to turn those hours of help they are giving away into actual productivity, they have to monetize the situations they are already in. For example, giving good advice over a cup of coffee. Or charging for your products instead of "helping out a friend." Or providing concrete feedback on a product or marketing idea. Every hour you help someone for free is an hour away from your kids or an hour you could have been charging your clients or business. Stop being too busy being helpful because if you don't stop, you will be helping everyone but yourself.

Take a look at your day-to-day schedule. Are you busy but not productive? If so, how? Now look at your ideas and the specific steps you wrote down in Pillar 4. Are the activities in your calendar helping you move toward that goal or not? If any of them are not directly contributing to your goal, they need to go. **Remember, one of the character traits of first-generation millionaires is that they value themselves. Practice that characteristic now by showing yourself that you value your time, energy, and money.** Don't waste those precious commodities on simply being busy. Be productive.

ACTION STEP

Take a look at your calendar, and identify the good but unproductive things listed there. You can have something on there that you think is productive, but if it doesn't directly help you reach your goal—if it doesn't contribute to your success in a linear way—take it off your calendar until you reach your goal. It *must* come off the calendar.

If you are doing things that keep you busy but don't help you reach your goal, then you are moving away from that very goal you set. Remember, **you need to prepare for your ideas**, but it only counts as preparing if your work, time, and resources contribute **to your goal**. If you don't need to do it, take it off your calendar. It's as simple as that.

PILLAR 5

BEING BUSY VERSUS BEING PRODUCTIVE

STREAMLINE YOUR CALENDAR

It's easy to **mistake** a busy schedule for productivity. Just because you have a lot of meetings, it doesn't mean you're getting things done. Maintaining **priorities** is the other important aspect to consider. Even if you have checks next to items on your to-do list, you need to make sure your **actions** line up with your priorities.

Being mindful of how you spend your time will dramatically increase the speed with which you meet your most coveted goals.

Your Assignment

Task 1. Go into your calendar right now. Review all of your meetings for the next seven days. If there are any meetings or tasks that **don't** align with your primary goals, move them to next week.

Task 2. Create some opportunity. Identify meetings that you've been putting off or haven't pursued that **do** align with your primary goals. Schedule them immediately—within the next seven days.

Now take a picture with the book and your filled-in answers, and tag me on Instagram and Twitter (@wimbrey),

as well as on Facebook and LinkedIn. Share your progress and cheer on others!

Be sure to add our hashtags:

#BAMM

#WIMBREY

#CoachJohnny

Avoiding Permanent Solutions for Temporary Situations

We've already talked about preparing, staying focused, and being productive. Now I want to turn your attention to a moment when preparation really matters: when you hear the word "no." There are always going to be nos, but people who understand wealth and are prepared for everything know that they can't make permanent decisions based on temporary situations. The best example of people who let a temporary state affect their permanent state are those who give up at the first sign of "no." That "no" is a temporary situation, but giving up is a permanent solution. Coming back from quitting is infinitely more work than if you just keep going, work through the no, and come out on the other side. Don't allow the temporary to rule your permanence.

You're going to get nos and setbacks. That's just a fact of life. I have gotten them. The highest-ranking members of my team have gotten them. Almost all of the most successful people I know have gotten them. But those successful people do not make permanent decisions based on negative emotions. Take me, for example. At 35, I was preparing businesses around the world. I was on almost every continent and in multiple countries establishing my brand. Then Greece's economy tanked, which was a major, major blow to my business there. I was unhappy. I was disappointed. But I wasn't devastated. I didn't look at what was happening in Greece and decide to close up shop everywhere and go home. I was prepared for something like this. I knew that if one country gave me issues, I could find those lost numbers elsewhere. And I did. If I hadn't been prepared, it would have been so easy to get upset, to give up, to be distracted from my larger goal. That's no way to live.

I want you to create a foundation for preparation and put yourself in a place where you understand that the good, the bad, and the ugly are coming. You need to know that curve balls are coming. The most important thing, however, is not that the curve ball is on its way. It's the fact that you are prepared to swing and hit when life throws the unpredictable.

I don't want you to give up on your dreams at the first setback because you are not mentally prepared and because you don't have an action plan in place for when it happens. The absolute most valuable asset of the millionaire mindset is that no one can take your mind unless you surrender it. Even if a setback or investment loss takes you back to zero, you will always have the power to get it back because your mindset is your greatest asset, not your bank account. Remember the millionaire mindset begins within, and as long as it's greater within, you will always be able to regain and sustain generational wealth.

Sometimes those setbacks have nothing to do with you. Things can go wrong that are completely out of your power. And when you feel wronged or lied to by a company, it is so easy to cut ties and walk away. I've seen it happen many times. And I can understand why people do that. They took a risk, they made an effort, they made an investment, and in the end, they felt like they had nothing left. It's so easy to take that feeling and literally run with it. But sometimes, seeing things through, giving them the room to right the wrong, can be worth the trouble.

I understand that human beings make mistakes. If I had given up on everyone who I felt made an error in judgment or tone, I would never be where I am today. Just recently, some of my partners and I were forced to choose between making a permanent decision for what we thought was going to be a temporary situation.

You never know when disaster will strike. Recently, a global pandemic derailed so many dreams. High school and college graduates who had jobs waiting for them no longer did. Small businesses closed all around us. Entire industries went under. It can be really hard to find a path forward when you see so many obstacles in your way. Helping yourself and saving yourself are more than just a mindset. They are about looking ahead and figuring out what you can do to protect yourself if the worst does happen.

In order to get ahead of a life-changing disaster, you can take the following precautions:

1. **Be prepared.** Personal development is always better used as preparation than as a last-minute solution in times of panic. Prepare and make the solutions second nature before you need to use them. You can't learn to swim while you are drowning. The same goes for personal development.

2. **Create strategic alliances with like-minded people.** No one of us is as powerful as *the many of us*. This is the reason I have been asking you to take a picture of yourself holding this book after every action step and tag me. By posting this photo, you can connect with other readers who are working to adopt this same mindset. Together you can become global brothers and sisters who are on the path of mastering the art of the millionaire mindset.

3. **Always live below your means.** Multiplying your financial success is never the reason to multiply your lifestyle. If you have to use a credit card as your only means to make a purchase of something you want, not need, you are living outside your means. If you don't have the money to back up that purchase, don't make the purchase. If it's unnecessary to purchase, then it's necessary that you walk away. There are many millionaires who lost everything during a pandemic or an economic downturn or a stock market crash because they thought only about summer during the summer. Mastering the art of becoming a first-generation millionaire is only evident when the generation that comes after you starts where you left off.

When you live within your means, you will be able to lessen the blow if things do happen out of your control. By doing this, you are thinking ahead and saving yourself from the unknown. By taking these extra steps, you are doing what the others around you are not. You are making sure that you will be able to get back up faster than anyone else.

And *when* disaster hits, not *if,* be sure to access your prepared stored assets, use your alliances for positive and strategic mental fortitude, and exercise your ability to thrive because you prepared. If you do these things, you won't be forced to liquidate to get back on track. If you prepare properly, you can hit the ground running as soon as possible.

———

For me, 2017 was my most character-building year as an entrepreneur—not because of what I made, but because of what I lost. I found myself in a situation where I was losing millions of dollars in revenue on a monthly basis for something that wasn't my fault. Every bit of it was traced back to a bad decision made by the company with which I'd partnered, and it had an incredible ripple effect on my revenue stream.

I had helped the company expand globally to the sum of well over $1 billion in revenue, a move that was pivotal to its success. I had brought in thousands of partners who now counted on this company for their own revenue streams. Even though I'd brought them success, this company made this failing financial decision without me—a decision that affected me and thousands of families around the globe. I was pissed off. I was hurt. I was betrayed. I also felt like I had to protect the many business partners and their families. I couldn't have the knee-jerk reaction that I wanted to because I knew my decision would affect more than just me. I had no idea what to do, but I did know this: I had nothing to lose by waiting and letting time pass, and I had everything to lose by making a hasty decision and walking away.

I gathered my executive team for this company and talked to them about what had happened. I gave it to them straight, but I did not withhold my feelings on the matter. That was a mistake. While I was honest, I was volunteering too much information as a leader. My panic, anger, and frustration caused some of my leaders to make a move without me. We were all equally upset at the same company, equally upset at the same circumstances, and we were equally owed money—some of us had been waiting more than a year for promised commissions that had multiplied into the millions. But they decided to take that anger and those feelings of betrayal and react permanently. They walked away.

I decided to wait it out. Virtually every leader who left early on regrets it to this day. They may have been right to walk away from such an underhanded company in that moment, but it was still not the right business move. Sometimes being right is not more important than what it could cost you. The ultimate payday was reserved for those who stayed with me, and I fought for what they were owed as much as I could. I eventually did make a move, when it was obvious there was no other option.

The art of mastering the millionaire mindset that will lead to many first-generation millionaires is to always remember that we are playing chess, not checkers. I want you to make moves with the end result in mind, and those moves will always require strategic preparation, strategic like-minded alliances that challenge you, and a strategy more for the future than for the present.

This is where faith in yourself, your team, your ideas, and your business come into play. It is easy to walk away from something if you don't have absolute faith in it. You can't have faith just when it's easy. You have to keep the faith when things get hard. Focus on exercising your *faith muscle* so it will be strong enough to withstand the times when you need it the most.

ACTION STEP

This chapter is about maintaining the heart and mind of a winner. I want you to be ready for that setback, no matter how big or surprising it is when it hits. I want you to work on building yourself up from the inside out. In order to do so, I want you to write about a moment in your life when you gave up, when you threw in the towel, when you just up and quit. Write it as if you are talking to yourself. Relive that moment, no matter how raw it makes you feel.

After you've poured your heart out, tell yourself what you could have done differently. What could you have done in the middle of that hell to turn that situation around? Looking back now, how would you have turned those bitter lemons into lemonade? Be honest with yourself.

Ultimately, I want you to be able to get out of a setback while staying on the path toward your goal in real time. I want you to prepare for the worst so that it doesn't floor you or completely derail you if it does happen. You don't want to find yourself improvising when disaster hits. Instead, have a plan in place, and be ready for the worst.

PILLAR 6

AVOIDING PERMANENT SOLUTIONS FOR TEMPORARY SITUATIONS

FIND A WAY THROUGH

Creating productive habits is critical to developing your **wealth mindset**. A habit you must adopt is having measured responses to **problem solving**—especially in times of distress.

On your path to wealth, you will meet roadblocks. You cannot give up. Don't make important decisions before **weighing** all your options. If you make a permanent decision in a temporary situation, opportunities and wealth will pass you by.

Your Assignment

I want you to **revisit** situations where you gave up when the road got tough.

Write down three of those situations and how you handled them at the time. Then, revisit those moments and identify **two ways** you could have approached the situation with a **wealth mindset**.

Temporary Situation 1: _____

New approach A: _____

New approach B: _____

Temporary Situation 2: _____

New approach A: _____

New approach B: _____

Temporary Situation 3: _____

New approach A: _____

New approach B: _____

Now take a picture with the book and your filled-in answers, and tag me on Instagram and Twitter (@wimbrey), as well as on Facebook and LinkedIn. Share your progress and cheer on others!

Be sure to add our hashtags:

#BAMM

#WIMBREY

#CoachJohnny

PART II
VISION VERSUS ILLUSION

This section goes into the nuts and bolts of your goals to show you how to create a mindset that gets results. You can sit there and think about what you would buy if you won the lottery, or you can get up, walk out the door, and actually buy a ticket for the first time in your life. You won't win anything unless you play the game.

Being a Wish Maker or a Risk Taker

This pillar is about the difference between a person who has vision and someone who lives in the world of illusions. The crux of this pillar is this: Are you a wish maker or a risk taker?

Let me illustrate this with a classic example. A few years back, the whole country was watching the lottery climb and climb. It reached $500 million, but no one won. It hit $700 million, and still no one won. Then it reached $900 million, and the news broke that someone got the entire pot. A single winner for almost $1 billion. It was amazing. I was with a friend of mine when we heard. He turned to me and said, "Man, I wish I had won that money. Can you imagine?" I asked him if he played the lottery, and he said no. I think I actually laughed out loud. I asked, "How are you going to win if you don't play?" Of course, he had no answer for me.

There is only one way to win the lottery: you have to buy a ticket. You have to participate in what you say you want. Remember back in Pillar 1 when I talked about what "participating in your own rescue" means? That is exactly what is happening here—even if you're doing something as far-fetched as playing the lottery. You won't get *anything* if you don't play the game. You have to take risks if you want any kind of reward.

I recently heard a statistic that just floored me. When on their deathbeds, the majority of elderly people said **their number one regret was that they didn't take more risks in their lives**. Their number *one* regret. Now I know these people are telling the truth; they are on their deathbeds. They have nothing to lose; they aren't going home. Why lie? So that made me ask, why is *that* their regret? I realized that it's all about the lifestyle people choose. It's how they live their lives, day by day and year by year. Not taking risks becomes a part of who they are— and this is something that is easy to regret when looking back. A person who *doesn't* take risks creates a lifestyle of someone who *never* takes risks. Taking a risk takes a moment, but not taking that risk becomes a lifestyle that leads to regret. If a person has a lifestyle of someone who doesn't take risks, I can guarantee that he or she won't be wealthy or successful. You must take risks.

I want to push you into the land of taking risks. In order to do so, let me talk about a time when I forced myself into taking risks and how it made me the person I am today. I knew at the age of 23 that I wanted to have my first six-figure year. I wanted to make $100,000 in 52 weeks. That was that. I was so specific in my calculations on how to go about doing this that I narrowed it down to the fact that I had to make at least two calls every day for 52 weeks to hit this goal.

In order to make sure I made those two calls every day, I took two coins and put them in my left pocket. Whenever I made a call, I moved a coin over from my left pocket to my right pocket. At the end of the day, those two coins *had* to move from the left to the right pocket; if they hadn't yet, I didn't let myself go to sleep. Now, there were days when I absolutely forgot to do this. On those days, I would take my jacket off at the end of the day, or hang up my pants, and one or two coins would fall out. That accountability set in immediately because I could not go to sleep. Why? **It was my job to participate in my own rescue.**

If I found a coin in my left pocket at the end of the day, no matter what time it was, I would force myself to make that phone call, to make that presentation, to make an exposure. I was not above using pity: "Ma'am, I am so sorry to be calling you this late, but it is mandatory that I do another sales call before I go to bed. I don't care if you are not interested. Please let me do a five-minute call right now, and then you can be on your way and I can go to sleep." It was a pity call, but it was still so impactful. Some honored me with the five minutes I requested because they simply felt sorry for me, and that is why I call it "the pity call." Many of the people I called honored the hustle; they honored my work ethic. And, eventually, many of them became clients.

I reached my goal that year thanks to those two little coins in my pocket. Those coins created accountability, and the accountability gave me the courage to take the risk. The purpose of this exercise is much greater than the objects used. I've seen people use two wristbands or two earrings. Whatever your personality type is and whatever visual will hold you accountable on a daily basis doesn't matter. The practice alone will lead you closer to the millionaire mindset.

I want you to think about where you can take risks in your life. For me, it was finding a way to force myself to make those cold calls every day. For you, it may be using this principle to track your daily advancement toward a project or goal, challenging yourself to exercise the mental muscle of meeting two new people every day, or implementing a positive impact shift on the planet every day.

Whatever your personal mission or goal is, when you attach that goal to a tangible, daily act of accountability, you are on a for-sure track to getting to that goal.

The most important muscle that you are flexing during this exercise is facing a new fear. You may not believe me when I say this, but I have had to get over my fear of talking to strangers. This was a huge problem for me, and it still is! To the world, I may be the guy who speaks on stages, is showcased on media outlets around the world, and affects millions through social media, but when it comes to one-on-one contact, I find myself being the quiet person looking down on the elevator floor or acting like I'm asleep with headphones on the airplane. When people find out who I am and what I do, they want to talk about it. I've always hated tooting my own horn to strangers, so I've thought that ignoring everyone around me was OK. Basically, hiding in plain sight became very comfortable for me, and I still struggle with this today.

But I also know that I need to work on this fear and flex the mental muscle of talking to strangers. Les Brown told me, "Johnny, you must be the message that you bring!" And that statement alone has caused me to implement a daily practice of having conversations with two total strangers with the intent of having them asking me what I do.

The reason I pushed myself directly into my fear of talking about myself with strangers was to create an opportunity to bring positive impact into those strangers' lives. I simply attached my goal to a purpose that was greater than my selfish fears of inconvenience and my shyness. Taking that risk has created incalculable positive results, and it has changed lives around the world. One way to face your fear is to make overcoming it purposeful and greater than your selfish desires. Focusing on the good is a major step toward the process of mastering the art of a millionaire mindset and becoming a first-generation millionaire.

Taking that risk is everything. Simply *wishing* for something will get you nothing. Taking a risk can give you everything. Take my mentee George, for example. A while back, I was in Spain, speaking for a company that I was partnering with. The company was operating on five continents, and George oversaw one part of its distribution for Europe and Asia. When I had first met him, he had no position in the company, but over the decade—under my guidance and mentorship—he carved out a position for himself. I was especially excited about the event because it meant I would finally be able to catch up with George. He was a great guy, and his wife had just had a baby. I was so proud of how far he had come in the company. I was getting amped up backstage, about to go live in front of 10,000 people, and seeing George walk up to me boosted my spirits that much more. As he came over to me, however, my smile faded when I saw his worried expression. He asked to speak to me, and I said yes immediately.

"What happened?" I asked.

"My bosses just yelled at me for something I didn't do. Like five minutes ago. I can't believe it."

"What?"

"I had to take the blame for dropping the ball when it wasn't my fault. I am now the face of this huge mistake, and I had nothing to do with it."

"George. If you had a magic wand, what would you want to happen? What do you want here?"

"I love the company. I love what we do. But I don't like taking the abuse when I did nothing wrong. I don't like being the scapegoat."

"How much do you not like it?" I asked him. "Do you dislike it to the point where you can put your foot down and say this can never happen again? Or is it not that painful yet?" He shrugged his shoulders in defeat. "If it's not that painful yet and you can deal with their treating you like this, you are just training them to continue to treat you like this. They are thinking to themselves *right now*, 'If George isn't going to fight back, we can keep using him as a scapegoat.'"

"Well, I don't want that," he shot back, perking up a bit.

"Here is my advice," I replied. "Set up a meeting at this event—right now—and you tell them, 'This can never happen again. I would be more than happy to walk away from this position if staying means that I have to keep taking the hits publicly for things that I did not do. However, I am more than happy to take responsibility if you give me the entire division.' If they are going to go off on you, you might as well take all the ownership for real."

George looked at me with disbelief. "You are telling me to go back to the people who *just* made me feel awful? I have a brand-new baby at home, and you are telling me to go back and threaten to quit?" He walked away, I went onstage, and I didn't see George for the rest of the evening. The next morning, however, he walked into breakfast, all smiles. "They gave the whole thing to me!"

When you don't feel like your value can win on its own merit, you will settle in life because you don't have the value to take the risk. Value yourself. Value your time and energy and ideas. **Building your value and exercising that muscle is a must if you want to build the character of a first-generation millionaire. No one will take a risk on you if you aren't willing to put yourself and your self-worth on the line.**

My protégé, Michael Jex, is the epitome of being a risk taker, not a wish maker. Right before I met Jex, he had been out of work for just over a year. He had been working in construction, but his employer lost its contract, and just like that, he lost his income. After that, he just couldn't find work. He thought about going back to the sales jobs he hated—retail stores and call centers—but the very idea turned his stomach. He told me later, "I couldn't stand the idea of working in a store again, but I didn't have a choice. My daughter had just turned one, and my lady was the only one working in our family. So I asked my friend to hook me up with a job at the AT&T store. But even with the personal reference, I still didn't get the job. Instead of being upset, I remember being perfectly calm in that moment after finding out. This was happening for a reason. I let it go."

A week later, he got a call from *another* friend of his who was already working with me. He wanted to join the company, but he didn't have the investment capital he needed. What he *did* have, however, was his unemployment check. Now, for him to take his unemployment check, something that was meant for diapers and rent, and invest it in himself is unheard of and a *serious* risk. That's not what unemployment checks are for. But Jex knew that this money would be the beginning of something great. He could have stuck with the status quo, but he chose to take the risk instead. He was participating in his own rescue.

Years after we started working together, I found out exactly how committed he was to joining my company. As Jex tells it: "The week before I heard about Johnny's company, I shattered my phone screen. It was completely unusable, and I knew I needed a new phone. By the time I heard about this opportunity, I had already spent my unemployment check on a new phone. For some reason, though, they hadn't charged my credit card or shipped the phone to me. When I saw that I had the chance to invest with Johnny, I had a decision to make: a working phone or this opportunity. In the end, it was easy. I called AT&T, canceled the order, and used the check to join the team. That check led to the millions I have today."

Most people would have used that unemployment check to do what society dictates as "right." Not Jex. He used 100 percent of it to start his business, and I coached him during the process. Now he is making millions on an international level. Jex is a true first-generation millionaire. He did the unthinkable. As Jex says, "Success for me didn't happen overnight. It took work. But I could have easily just used the phone as an excuse. I could have used my baby, or my single-income family as an excuse. I had a whole lot of reasons to *not* spend the check on this opportunity—it was the safer decision to make. But I always wanted this life. I had conversations with God about it. I felt that he was always testing me. He put so many obstacles in front of me, but when I saw this door, I was intent on kicking it open." Jex took his wishes, transformed them into reality with that risk, and has never looked back.

The risk doesn't have to be huge. You don't have to put all your chips on the table all the time. Sometimes, taking the risk just means putting out a hand to introduce yourself. I have found that the common denominator to any success can always be traced back to an introduction. Any merger, any acquisition, any partnership. If the common denominator to success is an introduction and you are not successful, I would immediately question how many people you are meeting. Not partnering with, not pitching—but meeting. If you want to narrow it down to what makes a person successful, focus on making those introductions. When you look at things that way, your motive is not to meet new clients or new business partners. It's just to meet more *people*.

There have been so many business decisions that I made in my life because I liked someone, and vice versa. Remember, the fact that I have so many people in my life and am constantly trying to meet more is ultimately the reason I met Les Brown. But I didn't meet him because I simply decided to one day. There were years of decisions to meet new people that led to that moment, and to this day I can still connect the dots to every single one that led me to Les Brown.

Don't sit with your back against the wall. Walk to the middle of the floor and start talking. Be a risk taker, not a wish maker. Here, the risk is meeting new people. The fear is rejection. You have to connect your fear to someone or something that motivates you, not demotivates you. I am afraid of losing everything and going back to the homeless shelter, so I use my fear as a motivator. I take the risk of meeting new people. How many introductions have you made in the last 24 hours? How many will you make in the 24 hours after reading that sentence? **All three characteristics of a first-generation millionaire come into play here: value, faith, and commitment.** Use all three to set your goals, establish what you need to make them happen, and then follow through without looking back.

ACTION STEP

I want you to use those same two coins from my story to reach your goals, to take more risks, to meet more people, and to hold yourself accountable. Find two coins and give each of them a task—a risk—that you must take every day in order to reach the goal in Pillar 3. (If you don't have pockets, use rubber bands on your wrists or something similar.) Be as specific and as precise as possible.

Now, do those two things every single day, and it will lead to new successes. I guarantee it. I have never had a client who hasn't found some form of perpetual success when he or she takes on the two-coin challenge. I know you will too.

PILLAR 7

BEING A WISH MAKER OR A RISK TAKER
TAKE DAILY RISKS

The difference between wish makers and risks takers is the belief that a **positive outcome** is truly possible.

Wishing is easy. **Taking risks** is a muscle you need to develop. Through the process of building this muscle, you'll realize that the upside of taking a risk if it pays off usually exceeds the pain of a moment of rejection or failure.

Your Assignment

Every day for the rest of this course, you will take **two risks**—and you will hold yourself accountable.

Find two items you can put in your left pocket—for example, two coins—**or** two items you can put on your left wrist—for example, two bracelets or rubber bands.

These two items will represent the risks you take each day. When you take a risk—make an important connection, make a sale, or something else—you can move one of those items to the right side.

Every night, when you get undressed, make sure you've accomplished those two things. And if you haven't, **do them before you go to bed!**

What are your accountability items going to be?

_____

_____

Now take a picture with the book and your filled-in answers, and tag me on Instagram and Twitter (@wimbrey), as well as on Facebook and LinkedIn. Share your progress and cheer on others!

Be sure to add our hashtags:

#BAMM

#WIMBREY

#CoachJohnny

Realizing Someone Else's Mentality Isn't Your Reality

n Pillar 8, I want to give you permission to supersize your goal. If you are like most people, you have pushed yourself to the understanding and thinking that **more is possible**. If your goal doesn't scare you, if it doesn't make people criticize you for what you think is possible, then it probably isn't big enough.

Let me give you an example from my own life. When I was 23 and about to get married, my mother-in-law-to-be moved into a brand-new, two-story house. I saw firsthand where my fiancée was living, and I knew for a fact that I did not want to carry her over the threshold of a house that was smaller and older than the one she had just left. For some unnecessary reason,

I felt obligated to maintain my future wife's lifestyle by taking her from one brand-new, two-story home to a new two-story home built from scratch and never lived in. My vision was honorable, but in reality, my thinking was a bit out there, to say the least. However, anyone who knows me knows that once I have a vision, I am pretty much wired to make it happen by any means necessary.

It was early 1998, only six months before our wedding day, and I had just turned 23 years old. I was sitting at my future mother-in-law's kitchen table with her husband, and she looked at me when I told her my plan, then sighed and said, "Johnny. This is not a starter home. This is not realistic. You need to do what everyone else does. You are getting married. *Be realistic.* Get a starter home." As I listened to her, my whole body just slumped. All the hopefulness and excitement left my face. I was crushed. I wanted to do something amazing for her daughter. I wanted to impress her daughter and her family. And the very person who motivated me to do this was now telling me that it wasn't realistic.

I want you to listen to me carefully: **someone else's mentality has nothing to do with your reality.** The house I wanted to give my wife wasn't an illusion. It was my vision. In my mind, it was already a reality for me. But the fact that it was my reality also meant that it was my responsibility to make it happen. Don't get me wrong; I'm not criticizing my mother-in-law. I love her. And she loves me. Her words didn't come from a place of malice but of love and concern. She was simply acting based on *her* reality, not mine.

Your vision is for you and you only. You don't need to waste your time convincing other people that it is sane or realistic or doable. You know it is doable because you have every intention of doing it. Someone else's opinion of your vision has nothing to do with your reality. You cannot make it your problem when someone else comes along and tells you that you are reaching too high, that you are crazy for wanting what you want, that you are going to regret this, or that they will never forgive you for leaving them behind.

Just as the state of Texas did for my insurance license, my mother-in-law didn't piss me off by telling me I couldn't do something. She *pissed me on* because she made my desire that much stronger to build that house. She made me realize that **no one is qualified to push my vision into reality except me**. So here is what I did: just like the settlers of Jericho, I walked around the land seven times, claiming this land as my own. People were watching, people were whispering, but I didn't care. I was declaring my vision, and no one could convince me that it wasn't going to happen.

Guess what? I got the land. I built the house. And I still own it today. In fact, when my wife and I moved into a house twice the size of that first house, I gave that house to my mother, where she and my stepfather, Tim, live today. Then, in 2016, my wife Crystal and I bought my mother-in-law—the same person who told me it was unrealistic to have a new, two-story house at the age of 23—*her own* brand-new, two-story house that she lives in to this day. Eventually those houses will be passed on to my daughters and son, who will become second-generation millionaires.

I was never upset at my mother-in-law. I wasn't upset at the doubt she was throwing at me. I simply didn't allow her vision to become my vision. Because it was my responsibility to push my vision into action. I had to participate in my own rescue. That goes the same for you.

The point that I want you to take away from the story is that even people who love you will try to limit your vision to protect you. They are not necessarily coming from a place of ill will. They're coming from a place of genuine love. You cannot allow even genuine love from people only trying to protect you to ultimately hold you back from your vision that you have for yourself. Never allow others to create your world for you because they will always create it too small. It is your responsibility alone to know how great your vision is, and it is your responsibility to bust your ass until it becomes a true manifestation.

You are going to run into a lot of people in your life who may try to stop you from doing what you know is best for you. They will try and say that you are reaching too high, or trying too hard, or that you will fall flat on your face and end up lower than you are now. It is going to be hard to hear that, especially from people you love.

When you find yourself in one of these conversations, I want you to do the following:

1. **Remember, other people's opinion of you should never dictate your reality.** Their personal beliefs cannot become your limited realities. Disqualify anyone's words that contradict your personal beliefs and where you are headed.

2. **Don't make them the enemy. Make their words your fuel.** I believe Frank Sinatra when he said revenge is all

out massive success. Your naysayers should be **shut up** by your **moving up,** not by your **speaking up.**

3. **Establish your WHY in everything you set out to do and accomplish.** Make sure that your WHY is greater than you. When the purpose is a greater than you yourself, it is more likely that you will never walk away from it. Someone's no will not interrupt your WHY if your WHY is rooted in greatness and a purpose that benefits others beyond you. Attach your goals to a purpose.

4. **Force yourself to constantly be surrounded around empowering information (like this book).** This is especially important when you are in the midst of moving toward your greatness. The music determines the dance. Any person, place, or thing that you allow to interrupt your inner music can be catastrophic to your purpose. We will discuss this later in the book in great detail.

Saying, doing, and thinking these things will ensure that the others' mentality isn't changing your reality. Focus on your vision and purpose, and disqualify any voice that confuses either. All your creativity and energy must be aimed toward your purpose. Shut them up with action and success, not a response, and stand firm and be extremely laser focused on your WHY. Be prepared by filling yourself up with positive reinforcements and voices that empower you from the inside out. Empower zero voices to interrupt your destiny. Make sure that you are always focused on your vision for yourself, not on what others may see when they look at you. It is the only way you will continue to participate in your own rescue. If you let others dictate what you do, you have already strayed from your path forward.

Not only do I expect this mentality for myself, I expect it for those around me. Even the ones I look up to. *Especially* the ones I look up to. In 2018, I decided I wanted to expand my business. In late June 2018, I launched Wimbrey Training Systems away from my home for the first time since we launched in 2006. I already had created multimillion-dollar businesses, but I wanted to create a legacy company. I knew it was time to set up shop in an office, hire a staff, and start expanding outward.

When I realized that this was what I wanted, I knew I didn't need someone to just run my team. I needed someone who would be a true partner. So I went to visit my friend Derek Williams. Derek and I have known each other for decades. I have gone to him for advice, support, and comfort more times than I can even remember. I knew he would give it to me straight.

To me, Derek has always been the picture of success. He was an executive at Johnson & Johnson for years. When I was a teenager, he was my first exposure to success—always the classic sitcom dad. He was the first person to take me to New York City. He was the first person to take me to Hawaii. I saw my first bit of luxury with Derek. I looked up to him. When we were teenagers, my friends and I would go to his house and dream build; being around him would just stretch my mind. I knew talking to him would help me through this transition. After talking about what I wanted to do, we decided to work together. I needed Derek as my right-hand man.

Derek and I chose our new office building together. He was nervous about going so big right off the bat, but I had faith in him, and us. We took the largest office in the entire building, and within our first two weeks, we were profitable. Within our first 90 days, we were profitable beyond a year's worth of production. Just as Derek used to stretch me—to get me outside of my comfort zone, forcing me to see beyond my abilities—now I had the chance to do the exact same thing for him. I didn't want him to be constrained by what he thought was "reasonable." I wanted him to be fearful of the risk we were taking when we signed the lease, but I wanted that fear to motivate him to take more risks—and it did. **He regrew his faith muscle the day we agreed to take that office. He gained faith in himself, faith in my company, and faith that creating his own reality outside of others' mentalities was the only way to be successful.**

ACTION STEP

Remember how I wanted you to find one person to hold you accountable? Here, I want you to take it up several notches. I want you to take the huge step and the enormous risk of sharing your goal—sharing your vision—with as many people as you can. Here's the catch: I want you to tell enough people that some of them start trying to discourage you. If you're lucky, the people who love you the most and are closest to you will be the ones who cast the most doubt on your dreams.

"That's crazy, Johnny," you may say. "Why would you want that for me?" I don't want you to suffer, but I want to *piss you on.* I want you to exercise your faith muscle, that essential key in your character for becoming a first-generation millionaire. I need someone to say, "No, it won't work." I need people you care about, people who care about you, to try to destroy your vision. Not because they don't love you; in fact, they are likely to say these things to protect you. But I want you to feel that pain because you have to understand on a personal and emotional level that other people's mentality cannot become your reality. **You cannot handle all this nay-saying if you don't have faith in your dream. Use these negative opinions to build up that faith and strengthen your character.**

You are just starting out. If you can't handle the doubt, the rejection, and the naysayers at this stage in the game, there is no way you will succeed in becoming a first-generation millionaire. You will hear more nos all the way to the top, and the stakes will just get higher and higher. *Now* is the time to learn how to make sure that they don't interfere with what you want and how you work toward your goals.

PILLAR 8

REALIZING SOMEONE ELSE'S MENTALITY ISN'T YOUR REALITY
CREATE OPPORTUNITIES

You can judge the size of your **character** by the size of the **obstacles** you overcome.

Criticism is part of the job. It's actually an important part too. This is true for two reasons:

1. If you are truly on a path toward wealth, you need to develop **grit**. Become a fighter for your ideas and instincts—don't let external opinions derail you.

2. Goals can't be achieved in a vacuum. Sometimes you have to put yourself **out there** to meet the right people and brainstorm solutions. This is a habit of a visionary.

Your Assignment

Show me you can handle the **heat**. Select an idea from your prioritized list from Pillar 4, and **share it** with two of the new connections you made in Pillar 2.

The goal of this exercise is to be strategic and deliberate. After you choose the idea you want to pursue, **identify** contacts who you believe can provide relevant insight or partnership opportunities.

Remember your **grit**. Reach out to as many contacts as needed to accomplish your two discussions. Some may reject or discourage you. Push past them.

Your Goal (from Pillar 4) _____

- Connection 1: _____

- Connection 2: _____

Now take a picture with the book and your filled-in answers, and tag me on Instagram and Twitter (@wimbrey), as well as on Facebook and LinkedIn. Share your progress and cheer on others!

Be sure to add our hashtags:

#BAMM

#WIMBREY

#CoachJohnny

Finding the Fear

N ow that you've told everyone about your plans, now that you have those closest to you saying you can't do it, now that you have built up that faith in yourself, I want to turn the conversation back to commitment. Commitment is one of the essential keys of your character, and you need to ensure that you have what it takes to see your goals through to fruition.

What I'm about to say to you right now is without a doubt strategically designed to shock you and force you out of your comfort zone. It is human nature to give something your full attention when the information makes you uncomfortable. You have made it this far, and I congratulate you, but, hey, let's get a little crazy.

Starting right now—this very second—I want you to have the dedication of a severe drug addict. Unfortunately, this point is coming from firsthand knowledge and experiences that I have seen with my own eyes. Growing up where I did meant that I saw too many people succumb to a drug addiction. I know first-hand what drugs can do to a person. A drug addict wakes up every day with one goal in mind: to get high. To see a person start every day from ground zero and still accomplish his or her number one goal, which is to self-destruct by getting high, was my first exposure as a teenager to the "whatever-it-takes" type of mindset. It was the highest form of "never give up" that I had ever seen.

Think about it. Drug addicts wake up every day knowing they are going to get high that day. They know that no matter what, they are going to find drugs and use them. The fear of not getting high that day is more powerful than the fear of not eating. Imagine tapping into that level of fear when it comes to your not creating and leaving behind your success and generational wealth. Nothing is going to stop them in their journey. Remember, they may start their day with absolutely nothing—no job, no family, no money, no home. Even then, they still have the dedication to get high that day and every foreseeable day in the future.

Of course, I don't want you to break the law to reach your goals, but I do want you to understand that waking up with zero doesn't mean you can't still hit your goal every day. Do you have the vision, dedication, and commitment to make *any* dream a reality? Is it truly possible to succeed regardless of your circumstances? The answer to that lies within our personal definition of success.

We all know that there are people who are in very adverse situations who still decide to win every day by hitting their goal through any means necessary. Now the real question is, what's your excuse that you have told yourself time and time again for why being a first-generation millionaire is not possible for you? And while you are entertaining your excuses, remember this: people at ground zero have already started their day with nothing and will—sadly, somehow and someway—successfully self-sabotage themselves while you are still contemplating your limitations and building a wall of excuses.

I want you to understand that my personal drive as a young adult was the fear that my children's first memory in life would be pain, rejection, and poverty, as mine was. That *fear* was my driving factor. I never wanted to be a millionaire. That was never my primary goal. All I wanted was to leave a legacy for my children so that they would never feel the pain I have felt. I woke up every day and worked hard for something that was much greater than I would ever be, something that was much greater than numbers in a bank account. I worked for something that would outlive me. I worked for my legacy.

It is written in ancient biblical scriptures, "A good man will leave an inheritance for his children's children." The bottom line was that I was fearful of not being called a **good man** when I closed my eyes for the final time. I ran toward my fears to redefine the legacy of the name Wimbrey, and that came before food itself or anything else, for that matter.

In order to reach that level of drive, you need to first look at your biggest fear. My biggest fear is going back to a homeless shelter. My first memory is having a refrigerator door slammed in my face at three years old. I was reaching for some milk, something I had done often at home. What I didn't know at the time was that I wasn't at home. I was at a homeless shelter, reaching into a communal fridge, and that milk belonged to another family.

I will never forget the shock, embarrassment, and pain of that door closing on me. I am more afraid of going back to that shelter than I am of holding out my hand and pitching the craziest ideas, standing on the biggest stages, or asking for that next opportunity. If you are going to have the commitment you need to truly succeed, you must first face the thing that you fear the most. Pinpoint that fear and say it out loud. Write it down. Tell someone else. Bring that fear to the surface so you can tap into it every day.

Most people allow their fear to become the limiting key factor that causes them to never take a step toward their destiny. I want to teach you how to use fear to drive you and to motivate you. When you find yourself running away from something, I want you to keep in mind that you're also running toward something.

A true champion of any kind knows that running toward a known fear is more rewarding than running toward the *comfort zone of mediocrity*. I have had the incredible honor of interviewing global giants of their particular industries, from professional athletes, multibillion-dollar-producing entrepreneurs, award-winning international entertainers, and many more respected high-level personalities. Through all those conversations, I have found that the common denominator for those who massively succeed is that they are motivated by their known fears.

I want to share a story of another young man who harnessed his fear. Another one of my mentees from Brooklyn. I met him when I was in New York City back in 2012 doing a wealth seminar. The seminar was for people who wanted to significantly increase their income by learning how to succeed as a new entrepreneur. The night before, I sponsored a qualification-only social. That meant that you couldn't just walk in off the street and join the party. You had to qualify to be in the room.

It was very clear that the night before the seminar, I would hold a private social gathering for people who had made the cut. It was a small group, and one of my top-level leaders told me that there was a guy he wanted to bring into the room to meet me. Even though he knew that this young man hadn't qualified to be there, my top-level leader was asking me to meet him. It would be worth my time, he assured me. I told him that I trusted his judgment, but it was on him. He was taking the risk by bringing him and diluting the personal up-close mentorship earned by those who qualified.

My top-level leader waved to someone, and suddenly the unqualified guy walked in. He was young, a boxer, and straight from the streets. He had an attitude that he wore on his sleeve. He also worked for a well-known shipping and delivery company, but, as many do, he had a side hustle delivering illegal packages that put his life in danger every day. I would later find out that his day job was a cover-up for his money hustle, and he wanted out of that life. As soon as we met, he started looking me up and down, sizing me up. I could see that he was thinking, "Are you the real deal?" He immediately started asking me questions without reservations; he was not intimidated at all. He was respectful with his skepticism, though, and he quickly started to grow on me. Despite the rough exterior, I was impressed. This guy clearly had the confidence and brains he needed to go far. I asked him if he was coming to the training tomorrow.

"Na, man. I can't make it."

I looked at my leader and raised an eyebrow at him. "You brought a guy here who isn't even coming to the training tomorrow? He's not even *that* committed?"

His excuses started when he saw my energy change. He said, "I need to be at work at 6 a.m."

"I don't care what you have to do. If you come to this training tomorrow, I promise you, your life will never be the same." I could tell he was intrigued. He turned back to my leader at the time, and they started talking quietly to each other. I said my good-byes, shook his hand, and moved on to the next group of people. As I saw him walk out a few minutes later, I was convinced I would never see him again.

At about seven o'clock the next morning, as I normally do, I came a few hours early to walk the room to make last-minute adjustments and to make sure everything was in order for the upcoming seminar. As I was walking in, guess who I saw: the young street kid boxer from Bed-Stuy Brooklyn. He was the first person there waiting.

"You made it! Your boss let you come?" I asked.

"Na." he said.

"So, you called in sick?"

"Na. I just quit." He had quit his job. He had walked away from that life forever, and he never once looked back. The fear he found was the fear of missing out on something big, something that could change his life. He used that fear to walk into his job at six in the morning and hand in his uniform.

He used the fear of missing out on his big break to push him to take the risk of not going to work (which I actually don't recommend, but who am I to push my opinion on to his reality?).

The result? He transformed himself. That fear of missing out has pushed him to say yes to so many things over the years, and it has opened him up to the most amazing opportunities. Needless to say, he would likely still be dropping off packages if the fear hadn't pushed him toward something bigger.

Within five years from that date, this young street kid proved to us all that he was the real deal and had what it took to give himself to the journey of becoming a first-generation millionaire. Do you? Answer that question truthfully. If you don't have what it takes, stop now and go reread the introduction and get back into a mindset that allows you to give your whole self to this cause. If you do have what it takes, keep reading and work on this pillar's action step.

ACTION STEP

Now that you have determined your fear and have your motivation and commitment in place, I want you to put those feelings into tangible actions starting today. I want you to put down this book, get up, leave your house, and go make some introductions that bring you closer to your goals. Every single deal—be it swapping baseball cards or multibillion-dollar mergers—starts with an introduction and a handshake.

I want you to get out and introduce yourself to at least three people. Maybe it's a mentor you thought was out of your reach, maybe it's someone in your field you have wanted to pitch for ages, maybe it's that "maybe" that you haven't chased down yet. I want that fear to motivate you. I want you to push yourself into the deep end of the pool, into the fire.

When you find yourself arguing for your limitations, I want you to remember the people at ground zero who start their daily process of succeeding another day with no evidence of when, how, or what, but they still start. This is your journey. This is your life, becoming a first-generation millionaire is your God-given obligation.

PILLAR 9

FINDING THE FEAR
ALWAYS BE HUNGRY TO CONNECT

Previously, we talked about grit. You have to be willing to stick it out even when the road gets rough.

Now, we're talking about **hunger**. We're talking about **fear**. You must be driven to create wealth. You've made it this far, so that shows dedication—but now let's flex some real drive.

Making **connections** is one of the first things we discussed. I'm bringing it back now because the strength and size of your **personal network** reflects the breadth of opportunities you'll have on this path toward wealth.

Your Assignment

Make **three** new connections. Not in the digital world. Make them in real life, **face-to-face**. Find three people you'd like to have coffee, lunch, dinner, or drinks with, and set it up today. They can be people you already know but haven't made a real bond with, or they can be people you've just met.

You don't have to meet them all today, but you must have **confirmed meetings** with them on your calendar before the end of the day.

Your new connection 1 (name): _____

Date of meeting: _____

Your new connection 2 (name): _____

Date of meeting: _____

Your new connection 3 (name): _____

Date of meeting: _____

Now take a picture with the book and your filled-in answers, and tag me on Instagram and Twitter (@wimbrey), as well as on Facebook and LinkedIn. Share your progress and cheer on others!

Be sure to add our hashtags:

#BAMM

#WIMBREY

#CoachJohnny

PART III
FRIENDS VERSUS FOES

My definition of a *friend* is "a person, place, or thing that pushes you toward your goal." A *foe* is "a person, place, or thing that pushes you away from your goal." So, for example, a foe can be your job or your house. A friend can be your neighborhood or your education level. In the context of this book, friends and foes are not the people you grew up with or your competition for your next promotion. They are instead friends and foes to your goals and the very idea of your success.

So, to be successful, you must first identify these friends and foes in everything you do as you take steps toward meeting each and every goal on your way to larger success. Before you take one more step, I want you to sit down and think about your friends and foes because you will never master the idea of wealth and becoming a first-generation millionaire without knowing who or what is working for or against you.

Conducting a Self-Inventory to Find Your Friends and Foes

When I was younger, I worked in a fast-food joint, flipping burgers and making shakes. It was a fun job. I got to get on the microphone and yell back orders as well as let my personality fly over the loudspeakers, and I had a great group of people around me. All in all, I enjoyed it. But four times a year, we all had to do something I absolutely despised: INVENTORY. I hated it. Every quarter, like clockwork, we would have to do a complete, extreme, itemized inventory.

Every ketchup packet, every bun, every straw, and every bottle of syrup had to be accounted for. We had to see what could be used and what needed to be thrown away. Even if we were throwing something away, my manager would want to know what it was and how much we were tossing. She understood that in order to maintain success, the business had to take account of all the things that were helping the restaurant and all the things that were hurting the bottom line.

Just like every successful business, you too have to do an inventory, but this one is an inventory of yourself. You need to do this so you can become successful and maintain that high level of success.

Slow down. Take your time with this. It won't be simple, and it won't be easy. It is one of the most important things you will do on this journey to becoming a first-generation millionaire. Consider it mandatory for success. I've done it myself, and sometimes you learn things about yourself that you don't particularly like, which is extremely important to take account of. For me, it was realizing that I had to take a season of separation from my childhood friends when I first started to become very successful—not because of anything they were saying or doing but because of the way I was acting around them.

I was acting a certain way around my childhood friends that wasn't who I wanted to be then or in the future. You see, when I began finding success onstage, earning money, and making a name for myself, I realized that I was keeping that part of my life hidden whenever I went back to the old neighborhood to see my childhood friends. (For the sake of clarity, I am going to call these friends "my boys" so you don't confuse them with the formal definition of *friends*—people, places, or things that are pushing you toward your goal.) I morphed back into "fun Johnny" and channeled that *Fresh Prince of Bel-Air* attitude that everyone loved so much. But that wasn't entirely who I was anymore. Now I was also "professional Johnny," someone people looked up to and respected. Instead of letting them see more of the "professional Johnny," I hid my success so I could be "fun Johnny" around them.

I started looking closely at my behavior. Why was I doing this? Was this a liability or an asset for me? As you perform a self-inventory, you must take account for every liability and every asset. An asset is something adding toward your success goals, and a liability is anything that takes away or moves you further from your goals. If it was a liability, I needed to know how and why, so that when I repeated this pattern down the road, I could recognize it quickly and act accordingly. **I didn't want my liability to kick my assets**, which was sure to happen if I ignored the liabilities and let them take over.

Let me be clear: my boys weren't my foes. I just needed to take a step back to figure out what was happening. I acted one way around the people who paid me to show them how to succeed and a completely different way around the people who have known me since I was a teenager. I felt a battle waging between the past and the present, and I didn't know how to balance who I was and who I was becoming.

In order to find the answer to that question, I first needed to identify the foe. I decided anything that didn't allow me to be the new me was a foe. If it wasn't pushing me toward my destiny, it was a foe. And, in this particular situation, I was the foe. I had to identify that fact so I could take a season of separation from these situations to get back on track again. I knew this was important. The danger of not identifying the foe in yourself is probably more dangerous than not identifying an exterior foe.

I thought my problem was that I wanted to be the high school, early 1990s' teenage Johnny with these guys, even though they were seeing my new lifestyle. I finally figured out that I wasn't worried about being liked or not. I was worried about coming across as a Mr. Know-It-All. Everyone else had no problem talking about their own successes, but because mine were so entrenched in global seminars about making money and teaching success principles, I didn't feel comfortable. But my actions and attitude were actually robbing them of their own potential. I could have helped them, but I didn't. I took a step back, recognized why this was happening, and then discarded it from my life. For a time. I am still dealing with this issue today.

I still hang out with my boys—our relationships haven't changed—but I don't know how to be 100-percent comfortable when I talk about money and success when we are all together. I find that instead of talking openly about business when we are all hanging out, they pull me aside and have one-on-one conversations with me. They all know what I have been up to. But even though they see me with Steve Harvey, or in pictures with Oprah, or at the White House with Emmitt Smith, they treat me the same way they did when we were all hanging out in high school. And I love them for it. But it's not fair to them that they need to go out of their way to ask for help. When I see this enemy within me once again, then once again, I have to take inventory of myself.

Even today, I continue to take inventory of this part of me. However, instead of a season of separation so I can figure it out, now I use the inventory I took way back when, recognize what is happening again, and change my behavior accordingly. Perhaps this means having a monthly breakfast where my boys can pick my brain or taking the time to step back and have everyone ask questions of each other based on our individual strengths. I still haven't found the perfect answer yet, but because I have already taken inventory of this foe and personal liability, I recognize it immediately when it rears its head again.

Performing self-inventory is not something that you do once and then never think about again. It is something that you do all the time. When you understand the inventory that's inside you, your assets and the liabilities that live within you and all around you, it empowers you to adjust and adapt **in the now**. My mentor Les Brown taught me, "Johnny **you don't know what you don't know.**" Not knowing your inventory of personal assets versus your inventory of personal liabilities puts you at a major personal disadvantage in any kind of fight.

Mentally compartmentalizing your personal liabilities and identifying your personal foes places you in position for far greater opportunities for perpetual victories. Remember, it is better to be prepared and never called than it is to be called and not prepared. Self-inventory is about future preparation for the unpredictable that life throws at us all. The ability to respond to life in the now is reserved for those who prepared in advance. Self-inventory and identifying your friends and your foes *before the battle* is mandatory for anyone who desires to master the mindset of a first-generation millionaire.

If you find this exercise easy, I promise you are doing it incorrectly. If you conduct your self-inventory in the truly right way, it should be challenging and very emotional. You must face and uncover every asset and every liability if you truly want legacy wealth. There are many people whom I have helped become massively successful who lost it all because self-inventory was not a priority above becoming wealthy.

Remember, the mindset of a first-generation millionaire is that you create the wealth. The wealth does not create you. A true in-depth dive into self-inventory allows you to build a strong foundation of great character. One of my golden rules for the mindset of a first-generation millionaire is that you never compromise your character for financial or public gain. Success and wealth attract temptations that most people would be devoured by, but those who master this exercise of self-inventory will have far more victories than they do losses because they know who they are from the inside out.

Remember, life happens to us all. What happens *to us* is never as important as what we allow to happen *in us*. This chapter is designed to fortify you for when life happens. Not if, but when.

ACTION STEP

Your ability to identify friends or foes quickly and efficiently could make you or cost you millions. Think carefully about everything and everyone you have interacted with since you started reading this book. Now, identify all the **people**, **places**, and **things** that are holding you back from your goal of being a first-generation millionaire.

What are some of the conversations you've had that made you rethink your goals? What are the places you went to that made you feel like you were not going to succeed? If people want to quit smoking, they can't go around with a pack of cigarettes in their pocket. Just like a smoker who wants to quit, you have to flush all of those loose cigarettes, even the ones in your backup, emergency stash. You have to get rid of *all* the foes of your goals, no matter how hard it is.

Every conversation you have is either complementing your goal or hindering your success. I am hereby mandating that you sacrifice and eliminate anything in your life that is holding you back while you are on this journey to becoming a first-generation millionaire. Before you turn the page, you *must* determine your friends and foes. You cannot move forward in the book until you do this.

PILLAR 10

CONDUCTING A SELF-INVENTORY
TO FIND YOUR FRIENDS AND FOES
TAKE AN INVENTORY

On the path toward any goal, there will be **external forces** in your path. You must determine whether those forces are your friends or your foes.

It's your job to stay **firm** in your pursuits. It is also your responsibility to be prepared to identify and neutralize obstacles or unproductive elements before they affect your progress.

Your Assignment

Name **five things** that are holding you back. These foes can be people, places, things, or beliefs.

Then explain how each, deliberately or otherwise, **pushes you away** from your goals:

1. _____

2. _____

3. _____

4. _____

5. _____

Now take a picture with the book and your filled-in answers, and tag me on Instagram and Twitter (@wimbrey),

as well as on Facebook and LinkedIn. Share your progress and cheer on others!

Be sure to add our hashtags:

#BAMM

#WIMBREY

#CoachJohnny

Determining Your Instigators, Spectators, and Participators

Now we are going to talk about three types of people you will have in your life: **Instigators**, **Spectators**, and **Participators**. Recognizing which category those in your life fall into is crucial to success of any kind, especially when you are on your way to becoming a first-generation millionaire.

Instigators are people who just talk about making things happen. And that's all they are: *Just Talk*. They don't even have the tools to make things happen for themselves. They are always on the outside, tailgating in the parking lot while the big game is happening inside. Although they can't even see it firsthand, they feel qualified to talk about the game and to pass judgment on the players, and they are even opinionated about the spectators watching in the stands. These are people who talk about the problem—they throw gas on the problem—but they never have a solution.

They wonder what's going on in the meeting they were not invited to be in. They are the ones who put down a leader's or someone in authority's ideas, but they never offer any solutions or alternatives because they lack the qualifications. An Instigator will repeat a rumor with zero research on the facts. An Instigator's reward is to recruit other Instigators, which brings them personal power. They are not motivated by personal success. They are only motivated to clap for or insult others' successes or failures based on the Instigators' own perceived best interest. Do you know any Instigators? If so, start listing them now. Do any of the names that are popping into your head surprise you?

Spectators are similar to Instigators in that they are simply there to observe, but the difference here is that Spectators will at least get close enough to actually see what's going on firsthand. They will watch the game, and they are usually the ones telling the Instigators exactly what is happening. The Spectators clap when you win, but the moment you drop the ball—the moment you make a mistake—they are the same ones to tell you, "I told you it wouldn't work! I told you that you were a fool to even try!"

These people sit in the stands and on the sideline, shouting plays at the players, reveling in the points earned, and booing every time the game doesn't go their way. When the game is going in their favor, they are celebrating and chanting. Spectators are everywhere. Now write down the names of the Spectators in your life. How have they affected your actions? How do you feel about seeing their names on this list?

Then there are the **Participators**. One of the great, distinguishing characteristics of Participators is that they are not only *actually playing* in the game but they are also *prepared* for the game. Participators know that 90 percent of life is preparation; only 10 percent is the actual game. Participators are the ones on the field. They are the ones who have been training several hours a day, every day. They are the ones making the sacrifices. They are the only ones moving the ball.

One of the most incredible and typically not acknowledged attributes of Participators is that they understand there will be no game without the Instigators and Spectators. Instigators and Spectators do not show up for practice. They show up only to see the real game. The Participators understand that the Instigators' and Spectators' role is incredibly necessary in order for the Participators to play at maximum capacity. For the Participators, the ultimate revenge is their all-out massive success, nothing else.

Instigators and Spectators fall into the "foes" category when it comes to your goals whereas Participators are "friends" to these goals. You need Participators in your life if you are going to reach your goals. But more importantly, you need those Instigators and Spectators. Don't run them off. Use them to empower yourself and to better understand both their role and yours. Be prepared for their insults. Learn to let their negativity roll off your back.

Participators also know that they have to constantly stay in position. If you want to be a Participator for your goal, you can never look right or left. You must stay laser focused on your goal. If you let someone hurl insults at you and make you turn your head away from your goal, you are putting that goal in danger.

You have to stay focused. The moment you allow an Instigator or a Spectator to pull you out of focus, you become your own foe.

———

It's important to point out that there are Instigators and Spectators around you, but they are also inside you. You have to learn how to recognize these parts of yourself and your behavior before they become a liability. You *must* be able to exercise that power of perception in the now. Letting them take over your thoughts and behavior for even a second can have long-lasting, damaging results.

I have learned so much about being both an internal Instigator and Spectator that I can now see right away when I am doing it—and more importantly, I can stop myself from acting on it. How? Let me share a story to show this in action.

A few years ago, it was very popular for people to hold personal development "heat camps," where participants would go into tents in the desert to cleanse themselves and their minds and hopefully have business or personal revelations. I already thought these sessions were borderline unreasonable, but I really sat up and took notice when I heard that someone had died of heatstroke at one of these events. I shook my head in sorrow and disbelief. "Why in hell would someone need that experience to create a true breakthrough?" I thought to myself, as I picked up my phone to post my opinion on social media.

However, as soon as I had these critical thoughts, I realized I was being an Instigator. I said to myself, "Johnny, right now you are on the outside looking in. You haven't researched these events. You haven't researched this particular brand. And the person in question may have already been sick, frail, or old. You have no idea what happened." Having that ability to realize what role I was playing helped me to step away from Twitter and stop myself from gossiping about the event.

My action wouldn't have brought that person back, and my tweet wouldn't have helped the leader of the event in question. The only thing it would have done was make me look bad, and maybe it would have come back to haunt me once all the facts were out.

I want you to start doing the same. Stop yourself before you do something you will regret. Stop yourself before you yell at the parent volunteer about how the pick-up line at school is set up. Hold your tongue when you feel the Instigator or Spectator coming through.

If you don't have the ability to recognize these three people inside you and on the outside in your daily life, it can cost you millions of dollars and decades of progress. When you do identify them, ask yourself why you entertain them in your life. Is it to spare their feelings? To make it easier on those around you? Or is it because you are afraid of what you will lose if you cut them out? Take inventory and discard that inner-foe type of mindset. It is the only way to find the success you want.

Participators talk about solutions, not problems. They make things happen by addressing challenges with solutions. They are trained to ignore Instigators and Spectators. Regardless of what's going on around them and regardless of all the hype, they never get out of position.

Participators are team players. They understand that break-ing focus could bring harm to their fellow Participators. There is no time for foolishness. They are focused on making things hap-pen. You have the task of figuring out which of these three cat-egories you fall into. You must make your decision now, before you can move on.

Are you an Instigator, always finding yourself talking about things that are happening? Are you a Spectator, watching things happen from a distance? Are you a Participator in the game, focused on the end result and constantly bettering yourself by sharpening your skills and preparing to make things happen? The hard honest truth is that we are all one of these three per-sonalities in everything we do and or entertain. Knowledge is power, right? No. **Applied** knowledge is power! Your power is in your ability to identify *in the now*, and adjusting immedi-ately *when* (not *if*) you find yourself going down the path of an Instigator or Spectator. Self-correction immediately exercised is an obvious clue that you are beginning to master the mindset of a first-generation millionaire.

You will never learn to value yourself and your efforts if you let the Instigators and Spectators infect your life, your goals, and your mindset. It's time to determine who is a friend and who is a foe and definitively distance yourself from your foes. I am giving you permission to take control of that focus. You need it if you are going to become a first-generation mil-lionaire.

ACTION STEP

Think of everything you do, everyone you talk to, everywhere you go, and everything you touch on a daily basis. Who and what is in your life on a daily basis? Are you constantly covering for someone else's mistakes? Are you picking up work you don't need to be doing? Is your socializing getting in the way of your productivity? Are you wasting time being busy but not productive?

Once you have that list, categorize each item as an Instigator, Spectator, or Participator in your goal to becoming a first-generation millionaire. In looking back and categorizing this list, I want you to start flexing this muscle. Going forward, work on putting anything new in your life or in your journey into one of these three categories. Soon, it will be instantaneous. You will be able to recognize the Spectators and Instigators right off the bat and react to them accordingly. You will also be able to recognize Participators. Those Participators will help you reach your goal.

Have you ever heard the term "trimming the fat"? It's slang for cutting off and getting rid of and discarding anything that's hindering you from getting to the good meat. Becoming a first-generation millionaire is your Prime Grade A Meat, and anything attached to you that is holding you back is your fat. This chapter and the exercise that follows will get you to flex a new mental millionaire mindset muscle that most run from.

Your ability or inability to immediately effectively identify Participators can *make you* or *cost you* millions. The first-generation-millionaire mindset takeaway for this chapter is this: "From this day forward your mindset is either making you millions or it is costing you millions. There is no in-between." Adopting this way of thinking is an absolute game changer when it comes to meeting your expectations during this journey.

PILLAR 11

DETERMINING YOUR INSTIGATORS, SPECTATORS, AND PARTICIPATORS
INVENTORY YOUR INFLUENCES

Preparation and **accountability** are relevant throughout this course. In this lesson, we discuss the people closest to you and how they affect your progress.

As you've read, people in your life fall into three categories:

Instigators: They focus on the current reality. They are often the first to point out and linger on the problem, while putting little effort into the solution.

Spectators: These folks have no skin in the game but posture as if they do. They watch the game but don't play. We don't see a lick of loyalty in this type. They tend to be fair-weather friends.

Participators: These people make things happen. This is a rare breed but extremely useful to identify. They actively take part. Ninety percent of a Participator's effort is dedicated to prep and practice.

Your Assignment

List five of the closest and most important people in your life. Then describe which **type of person** they are and how they influence your goals:

Individual 1: _____

Personality type: _____

Individual 2: _____

Personality type: _____

Individual 3: _____

Personality type: _____

Individual 4: _____

Personality type: _____

Individual 5: _____

Personality type: _____

Now take a picture with the book and your filled-in answers, and tag me on Instagram and Twitter (@wimbrey), as well as on Facebook and LinkedIn (feel free to black out the names if you want to keep them private). Share your progress and cheer on others!

Be sure to add our hashtags:

#BAMM

#WIMBREY

#CoachJohnny

Becoming a Friend to Your Future Self—Mentally and Physically

N ow, we all know at this point that there are friends and foes of your goals all around you, but it's also important to remember that *you* have to be **a friend to your future self** if you want to succeed. Being your goal's own friend comes right back to participating in your own rescue. You can eliminate people, behaviors, and mentalities out of your life all you want, but all that work you've done to better yourself doesn't mean anything if you throw it all away in an instant. If you lose your temper once you have made it big, you could lose a company, a house, a fortune, and even a family. I know so many people who have worked their entire lives to build something only to watch it disappear due to a heated exchange in a meeting, a rash response to a troublesome customer, or the fact that they let their emotions get the best of them in a business setting.

In this pillar, I want you to start looking ahead. What will your life look like once you reach your goals? What will you have? And more importantly, what will you have to lose? From this moment forward, I want you to protect that future self of yours by choosing your actions carefully.

I want you to picture yourself in the house you want, driving the car you want, being able to give your children what they need when they need it. You may not have these things now, but I want you to comport yourself as if you do. Only then will you be able to be a friend to your future self.

Starting this very instant, I want you to go through life reacting to things not as if you have nothing to lose but as if you have *everything* to lose—because **you do**! I want you to internalize the fact that the actions you take now will affect your future self. Do you want to help that future version of you, or do you want to sabotage him or her? What happens to you in the future depends solely on how you act in your present.

As confident and mentally stable and strong as I would love to believe I am if you came up to me and suddenly slapped me across the face, at this point in my life I am about 99.9 percent sure I will probably slap you back. I am just not at a place in my life where I can simply turn the other cheek and wait for another slap. But here's the thing: the minute I slap you back, I need to take responsibility for my reaction.

If I were a whiner, I'd say something along the lines of, "He hit me first! He started it!" Which sounds exactly like what a child would say, right? Well, I can say that all I want; the courts don't care. I am working on turning that cheek because as I be-come more and more successful, I have more and more to lose. Because I have more to lose, I have to be laser focused on the en-vironments into which I walk. I can't start a fight with everyone who upsets me. I can't throw a tantrum if a waiter brings me the wrong type of soda. I can't bang my fists on the boardroom table if a deal is not going my way. I have to respond; I can't just react.

In 2018, I had the honor of being in a leadership class taught by Bishop T. D. Jakes. He taught from a very familiar passage in the Bible that I have heard quoted hundreds, if not thousands, of times. The way Bishop T. D. Jakes dissected this passage rocked the very foundation of my soul—I mean in a way that I walked out of that session a different person. His reference came from Corinthians I, Chapter 13, Verse 11, written by the apostle Paul: "When I was a child, I spoke like a child, I understood as a child, I thought like a child, but when I became a man *I put away childish things.*" Please understand that this is a scripture that I have been able to quote since I was a teenager so nothing about this scripture was new to me—at least that's what I thought.

If you notice above, I emphasized the words "*I put away.*" In this particular leadership session, that's what he focused on, those three words, and those three simple words would ul-timately change my outlook on my complete journey in life. There have been many times in my life when I have felt like people were honoring who I am now without honoring who I was before I got here, and I've never been OK with that. There are things that the old Johnny did that I massively regret today, but the truth is, I love that Johnny just as much as I love today's Johnny, if not more. And I had always thought that this par-ticular scripture was saying I needed to kill the old Johnny, but

Bishop T. D. Jakes released me from ever thinking or feeling that way again. How? Because he said that when you *put something away*, that's acknowledging you still know where it is and how to access it at any moment that you may need to.

The apostle in this scripture never said he destroyed the thinking of a child. Instead, he said he put his childish ways away. I cannot explain to you how much I needed that lesson. You see, I was never taught self-control as a child. I was taught fear and consequences, but not the benefits of self-control. Whenever I lost self-control as an adult, I felt the old Johnny surfacing. Feeling him again made me feel like I was not exactly where I thought I should be when it came to personal maturity. Now I know that is not the case. Instead, it just means that I have accessed something from my past that I put away, but I have the power to put it back where I found it—and by "it" I mean reacting instead of being responsible. I am sharing this with you because this is a personal place of struggle for me even to this day.

Life will throw you lots of curve balls, no matter how successful you are. I want you to practice swinging at them. I want you to know exactly how you are going to act. It's not the curve ball itself but how you respond to the curve ball that comes your way.

Every time I find myself reacting with emotion, I simply know that the old Johnny has slipped off the shelf, and if I want to truly continue to master the art of the millionaire mindset, it is my responsibility to clean up any mess and put him back on the shelf as fast as possible. *Responsibility* simply means the ability to respond. The hidden word is *able*, which means it's possible for all of us to respond instead of reacting. Reactions are the ways of a fool. Responsibilities are the ways of the wise. Wisdom is the application of knowledge. The opposite of wisdom is foolishness, which means you have knowledge but refuse to apply it. Prisons are full of people who reacted instead of responding. The more you have to lose, the less you can react.

When you find yourself *at the start* of a confrontation, remember these three things:

1. **Ask yourself the question, "What do I gain by being right?"** If the answer *only* feeds your ego, just walk away. It is more self-empowering to exercise the ability to experience a victory that only *you* realize than it is to publicly prove you are right. This is a mental muscle that is so rewarding once you give it a shot.

2. **Ask yourself the question, "What does this person have to gain, and what do I have to lose?"** If your loss potential is greater than his or her gain potential, that is evidence that you are in a no-win situation. Never argue with anyone who has nothing to lose. The loss exposure should be equal or greater for the opposing party.

3. **Ask yourself the question, "Am I strong enough to take control of my reactions?"** The answer is always yes. Remember, arguing with a fool in public will only force the public to determine who the fool is. Staying in a position of self-control will lead other powerful leaders to invite you into their circles.

Take a deep breath, and let those three items run through your mind, even if you have to step back and take a minute. It will be worth it in the long run. Your future self will thank you for not getting into this particular fight. It may be hard in the moment, but your thoughtfulness and poise will pay off in the long run.

Now, when you are actually *in the middle* of a heated confrontation, I want you to pause and do the following:

4. **Ask yourself, "What will being right profit me in this situation?"** What does their being right profit them? If they are in a position to gain more by proving you are wrong than you will profit for proving you are right, remove yourself from this risk exposure immediately.

5. **Ask yourself, "Am I the one who has the most to risk?"** If the answer is yes, leave immediately. Never stick around to feed your ego. Feeding your ego publicly is reserved for those on the path to nowhere.

6. **Ask yourself, "What is the absolute best end result that can come from this?"** If the best result is showing your ability to walk away, then exercise that option. The weak-minded naysayers don't matter, but the few in power that may witness your strength could open future doors of possibilities down the road. No one in power wants to partner with or give control to someone who lacks self-control.

The following two principles have probably saved me from losing millions:

1. Never argue with the fool in public because the public will never know which one is the fool.

2. The fools will always expose themselves so never interrupt them.

Whenever I think of responding versus reacting, I think of my 25-year-old self, driving down the street in my BMW convertible. I had just listened to a Tony Robbins audio recording about staying in control when—and you can't make this stuff up—someone in the next lane over flipped me off, cut me off, and drove off. In that moment, I realized that by doing this to me, he was elevating *my* importance in *his* life. He was making me number one. When he did that to me, I didn't do anything. I let him drive off and went about my day. I was being responsive and not reactive. If I had reacted and raced after him, I would have been telling *him* that he was number one in *my* life. I would have been elevating him. And no matter what I did that day, I would have been responsible for my actions.

Remember, it's not what happens *to* us. It's what happens *in* us when something happens *to* us. **It's how we interpret what happens to us and how we allow ourselves to react.** When adversity comes our way, do we inspect what we expect? Are we a friend or foe to our future selves? Are we participating in our own rescues? Are we thinking about the consequences of reacting over responding? No matter what you do, you either have to be responsible, or you react and then take responsibility for your actions. You might as well be responsible from the get-go. Learn how to be responsible now so you don't have to face the consequences of your actions when you have everything on the line.

"This is all well and good, Johnny," you may say, "but what does this have to do with becoming a millionaire?" It doesn't have anything to do with it. But it has everything to do with *staying* a millionaire. I don't want you to just *be* successful. I want you to *maintain* that success for decades to come. I want you to be able to pass it along to your children. If you work your tail off, get the business, earn the money, and achieve the success just to lose it all because of a reaction to adversity, all that work will have been for nothing. I want you to know how to respond to a problem before you ever even face it. I want you to act like everything is on the line because one day it very well could be, and the last thing you and I both want is for you to lose everything because you didn't prepare yourself to respond. You need to exercise this mental muscle now so it is ready for you to use down the road.

Think of your future self. How will you handle a day of disappointing meetings if you cannot handle someone cutting in line at Starbucks? Every day, I seek out small instances of adversity so that I can work my *response muscles* for when I see a real, consequential curve ball coming my way. If I stamp my feet and yell when someone is rude in the grocery store, how will I possibly be able to stop myself from doing that in the boardroom? I have trained (and continue to train) myself to act as if I have everything to lose all the time. Before you can achieve the massive successes you desire, you have to internalize the idea of responsibility and manage how you react to the world around you. Reactions are emotions; responsibility is power.

When someone writes a bad review or starts bad mouthing you to clients and business partners, I want you to respond *as if* you had dozens of employees who depended on you for a paycheck. How would you respond to disgruntled customers? I want you to take a measured approach and figure out why they are saying what they are saying. Don't just lash back at them. That may feel good *now*, but it will definitely not help you down the line. When someone trashes you or your business on social media, I want you to respond *as if* you already had achieved all the success you set out to achieve. **I want you to stand firm, master self-control, and choose your fights wisely.**

When my friend Holton Buggs first started making it big, he also started getting a lot of negative reactions on social media. His first reaction was to fight back online, to stand his ground. But as he kept doing this, he realized that the old Holton was calling the shots, not the new businessman he knew that he had to be. He stopped in his tracks and made a decision then and there: that he would never react from a place of anger. By changing how he reacted, he began practicing using those mental muscles, so the next times it happened, not only did he know exactly what he needed to do but it also got easier and easier for him to do it.

If people do bring you negative confrontation, I want you to be seen as the authority in control because that is how millionaires with much to lose act. They know how to pick their fights and walk away a winner every time. Learning how to pick my fights was something Les Brown taught me firsthand.

Years ago, a young lady in my field was approved to coauthor a book with me. She went through the process, and I invested in her chapter. We even printed the books. But then she pulled out of the deal at the last minute and wanted her money back. Well, I wasn't going to make any money on the book, but I wasn't ready to lose money, so I told her no. I had no problem doing this because I knew I was in the right. She had backed out. There was *no way* my stance was going to backfire on me. Not when I was *this* right about something. Well, she called her lawyers, and I called my mentor Les Brown.

It was in my nature to seek wisdom from my mentors, but in this case, I almost didn't because I was so sure that I was in the right. I didn't feel like I needed any advice. Boy, was I wrong.

"Johnny, you have to give her her money back" was the first thing Les said to me after I explained what happened.

"No way. I am not wrong here! She is!"

"It doesn't matter if you are wrong. If you fight her on this publicly, everyone will think that you need her money. That will be the perception. No matter what she says you did or didn't do or said or didn't say, you will be left defending yourself. That defense will take energy away from something good, something productive, something that could help you."

I knew in that moment that I needed to end this no matter the cost. I got her on the phone, and Les put it on speakerphone: "You are talking to Les Brown. Go ahead, Miss." As he was being nice to her and praising her speaking, my collar was getting hotter and hotter. How dare he be nice to her? How dare he give her things! But when it was all said and done, he said, "OK, we are going to give you your money back." And just like that, it went from me against her to us against her. Les used his credibility as currency because he was in the position to do so. After we hung up the phone, he told me, "It doesn't matter if you did it or not. If you can get rid of something based on your value, do it. Pick your fight." I was so focused on being right that I wasn't focused on the energy I would have spent fighting with her for that $2,500. Over the 10 years that followed, picking my fights saved me millions. **When things go wrong, don't go with them. Take the higher road.**

From this moment forward, I want you to operate in *as-if mode*. I want you to walk around, conduct business, and live your life *as if* you already had a global business that was worth millions. *As if* you had already reached your goals. *As if* you were already successful. Then, when you finally have success, you will already be a master at responding, not reacting. You will have the power and the ability to control your emotions and your behavior, allowing you to be a friend to your goals. When you react, you risk losing everything. **You cannot respond until you have faith in yourself and your ability to succeed. Success should be a foregone conclusion. Be faithful to your future self in your actions today.**

Before reading on, I want you to take a pause and do something for me. I want you to think about a time when you absolutely lost it—possibly in a very regrettable moment in your life. Write it down. Relive the emotion. Don't hold back. Now that you've done that, I want you to write about a moment when you stayed in control. Maybe your kids were around. Maybe your boss was around. Regardless of the situation, I bet you kept your cool because you had something to lose, whether it was the respect of your children or your job or whatever else you valued at the time.

Now take it a step further. Write down two more instances of when you reacted to something and two more instances of when you responded to something.

I want you to feel the reward of responsibility. I want you to exercise those mental muscles before the deals, money, and success start rolling in. Now is the time to position yourself for the future, when you will have everything to lose.

Don't read any more until you have done this. Your experience will be so much richer if you take the time to think about these two types of instances carefully and why you reacted the way you did.

———

My good friend and international motivational speaker Gary Eby always said, "Change is a door that can be opened only from the inside." People who react are trying to change other people through their actions. Do you think telling off the woman who doesn't pick up after her dog will make her change her actions? Probably not. You don't have that power. You have power over only your own actions.

In order to drive the idea home, I want you to think about an athlete on the field. A 300-pound American football player. A huge guy, full of contained power, ready to give his all. At the sound of a whistle—at the command of a "hike"—he will slam into the opposing team with every ounce of energy in his body. He is close enough to his opponent that they can spit on each other, close enough to insult family members and loved ones. He is doing everything he can to get into the heads of his opponents. His goal is to get the other team so riled up that they step out of line and get a penalty or are thrown out of the game. And they are doing the same thing to him.

The only thing that prevents him, his teammates, and the other team from completely losing control—the only thing that causes them to walk away in a split second—is a whistle. At the sound of the whistle, everyone steps back, self-control intact. Is it the power of the whistle? Is it the power of the referee who blows it? Or is it the power of the penalty?

The penalty is the only reason the player has the maturity and discipline to get up and walk away. If he doesn't keep his temper, energy, and anger under control, he is putting himself in jeopardy, and he is putting his team in jeopardy. How does the sound of the whistle keep him in check on the field? After years of conditioning, he knows that when he hears that whistle, he has to walk away from whatever insults are being thrown his way and get back into formation, or he will pay the price.

Now, that exact same player could be on the elevator with his girlfriend, lose control, and knock her out. That exact same player could feel someone step on his shoes in the club, lose his temper, and pull out a gun. It's the whistle that creates discipline. Without that whistle, he has a much harder time keeping that energy in check.

Football players have coaches on the field to help them control themselves, but very few have those same types of coaches in everyday life. A coach is meant to protect their players, even from themselves. You can't tell me these guys don't have discipline. They do. They just don't always know how to transfer that discipline to their everyday lives. Let me ask you: What are you allowing to condition you in *your* game of life? Can you condition yourself to live by the whistle and walk away from a situation that could cause you to be thrown out of the game, or do you start the brawl, take the bait, and be the one to get your whole team disqualified?

Every first-generation millionaire needs to prioritize learning to live by the whistle in every aspect of their lives. Remember, as Les Brown always says: "It is always better to be prepared and not called than it is to be called and not prepared." Success requires preparation with the hope of never having to exercise this extreme discipline, which in turn prevents extreme losses through penalties, whatever they may be.

I knew that I had to be ready when it was my time to face adversity. One of my biggest challenges came to me when I least expected it. It was not when I was in the boardroom or onstage or in the middle of negotiating a new partnership. It was when I was out for dinner with my wife.

My wife and I had just participated in an event in Plano, Texas, for the show *Black Love*, which was about successful couples in the African-American community. It had been featured on the Oprah Winfrey Network (OWN). We had been personally invited to attend the event by the multi-platinum-earning, Grammy-winning artist Kirk Franklin and his wife, Tammy. After the event, we happened to be across the street from Sambuca 360, a restaurant that Crystal and I both like and where I had hosted a few large events over the past several years. It occasionally had live jazz music, and since we both love jazz, we went in to see who was performing that night. When we walked in, we saw that all the best seats around the stage were reserved. I had started looking in the back when my wife called me over. She had found a high-top that was right in the action and didn't have a "reserved" sign on it. We sat down, ordered drinks from the waitress, and watched the musicians get ready for their set. After about 20 minutes, we were ready to order our second round of drinks and started looking at the menu.

Before we could even order our food, however, a man walked over. He explained that no one should have seated us there, that it was reserved for someone else, and that he would be happy to move us to another table. I listened to him calmly and then told him that we were good where we were. Neither of us wanted to give up our great seats, and we had already gotten our drinks. As soon as he heard my polite reply, he started getting agitated, so my wife pulled out her cell phone and start recording. (This was only a few weeks after the infamous Starbucks incident in Philadelphia in the spring of 2018.) He stormed over to another man, started talking excitedly and gesturing over to us so I started to record on my phone because his body language and gesturing was very bizarre, and I knew it would be my word against his. Then he came back in a huff.

"You've got to leave."

"Why?"

"Because I don't like you."

"Because you don't like me?"

I was being as cool as possible on the outside, but I was boiling inside. He told us we were trespassing, and I held up my drink as proof that we were paying customers. He told us we couldn't sit there because it was someone else's table, and I replied that it wasn't reserved. That's when he pulled out *his* phone—and called the police. He told them he had an "irate black guy" who was "refusing to pay his bill" and "refusing to leave." His last comment to the dispatcher chilled me to the bone: "And we don't know if he has a gun or not."

The old me would have lost my cool. I would have been yelling. I would have caused a scene. I would have likely caught the attention of the police. But I knew what I had on the line. My family. My reputation. My standing in the community. My business. Even my freedom. I had too much to lose to act a fool. Was I being discriminated against? Of course I was. But I couldn't let that injustice cloud my judgment in the moment.

We paid our bill and were walking outside when the cops arrived. They stormed past us and looked for the "irate" black guy who may or may not have had a gun. They didn't even give me a second look because I didn't fit the description of the picture that the manager had painted to get the Plano Police Department to storm in as if a robbery were taking place. I kept calm and rose above. A few days later, after the video went viral and was picked up by the news, the restaurant issued an apology to me. I didn't lose a thing.

Sambuca 360 went from having a four-star online rating to less than two stars. The video has over 1 million views on social media. Virtually every news outlet across the country—and many international markets—picked up the story. My staying in control created global visibility for me and my brand. The man's behavior cost the restaurant dearly.

Being reactive to every little (and big) thing is what whiners do. Being responsible for their own actions is what winners do. **I want you in the winner's circle all the time.**

The second part of this chapter will address how you must take care of your body. I want you to start respecting your body—thinking about what you eat, focusing on what you do to stay active, and considering what vices you indulge in. If you make bad health choices now, you are going to suffer the consequences later. I don't want that for you. I want you to live a long, healthy life, so that you can see all this hard work support your children and their children after them.

Being a friend to your future self doesn't just mean learning and practicing how to deal with adversity and saving yourself trouble down the line. It also means taking care of your body so that you are around to see your children and your children's children reap the benefits of your hard work.

Let me give you an example from my own life. Not about my business, but about my health.

When I was 21, my uncle—my namesake Johnny Dale Wimbrey, Sr.—died from a heart disease–related incident. My family members were shocked. In our minds, he was incredibly successful and incredibly healthy. Just a year before he died, in 1996, he had actually carried the Olympic torch through Fort Worth, Texas, on its way to Atlanta, Georgia, where Mohamed Ali would ultimately light the flame for the official Olympic Games. It just didn't make any sense to any of us. Within a year and a half of his passing, two more of my uncles died from heart disease. My father had his first stroke that same year. My father would ultimately have over two dozen more strokes and lose many physical capabilities including his ability to drive and walk. With all of this information, it's clear that heart disease used to run in my family. I say "used to" because I made sure that the streak of Wimbrey men dying at a young age from heart disease would end with me. I broke that chain. I broke that generational curse. I was a friend to my future self.

When I was 35, I took out a life insurance policy. Part of the process was a lengthy medical workup. The doctor at the agency called me the week after my checkup and told me that the company had to increase my rate because my cholesterol was too high. It was a sobering phone call because I saw firsthand what that could mean. I did not want to end up like many of the Wimbreys I had seen perish during my lifetime thus far. Those men had died suddenly before they were ready. I knew something needed to change.

I told the doctor that I exercised but that maybe I wasn't watching what I ate as closely as I should. He gave me two options: cholesterol-lowering drugs or a 90-day health challenge. I was at a crossroad. I could live as I had been living, take the drugs, and end it there. Or I could take the necessary steps to make a substantial change and be a friend to my future self. I chose the latter. I chose to destroy the high cholesterol. Not only did I exercise every day but I also cut out all meat from my diet for three years. As Les Brown says: "Nothing tastes as good as living." I made that my motto. I took control of my health, my future, and the future of my family. I had the choice to be a friend or foe to my own life. It was my responsibility to participate in my own rescue.

Speaking of participating in my own rescue, a lot of people look at me as if I am crazy when I tell them how much I spend on my own personal development. Seminars, books, and conferences add up. But to me, they are worth every penny. I have spent over $100,000 to spend time with industry leaders, giving myself the chance to learn and apply what I've learned to my own efforts.

Think about how much you have spent on movies, concerts, dinners out, and vacations. How easy it is for you to justify buying that third pair of sneakers or the sunglasses you have been eyeing. How many hours have you spent gossiping with your friends or scrolling around on the internet, especially social media platforms? How many hours have you spent learning sports statistics and watching college basketball?

Now, if your job is making or reviewing movies or concerts or sneakers or sunglasses, or if you are a gossip columnist or an NBA recruiter, then this is how you are productive. More power to you. But let's be real: most of us do not fall into those categories. If you are wasting your time, resources, and money on things that do not directly affect your success, then you are allowing those things to pull you away from your destiny. Don't give into the now. Invest in your future. Your future self won't remember what movie you saw on a Wednesday night, but she will thank you for saving up for that course, for studying for that test, for taking the time to make those few extra connections.

Never cease to invest in your internal and external personal development. The consistent development of your mind will become the universal key to unlock any door that you desire to walk through. The consistent upkeep and development of your body will be the deciding factor of whether you can run through that door or barely walk.

When I was a child, we watched Saturday morning cartoons. I remember very vividly one of the commercials that would come on multiple times during the morning. It was a commercial that promoted eating healthy. I am literally laughing right now because I can still hear it in my mind at the age of 45. This unidentifiable character would say these words to music: "You are what you eat from your head down to your feet." So simple and yet such a perfect example of common sense that is very uncommonly practiced. Who you are today is directly related to what you physically, mentally, and emotionally consume. You are what you eat, so what will it be? Will you fritter away your present and sacrifice your future, or will you invest in your future self now and reap the rewards down the road? **Prove to yourself that you value your future, and commit to seeing that feeling of value come to fruition.** Not everyone can do this. It is so easy to bargain your future away, bit by bit. If you aren't willing to make the commitment to your future self, you will never become a first-generation millionaire. Remember, the millionaire mindset begins within. When I made the sacrifice to stop eating meat for three years, that strength came from within, and ultimately the benefits were both internal and external.

Once you truly obtain the millionaire mindset, sacrificing temporary desires becomes a daily practice, and anything that is a daily practice will ultimately become a simple lifestyle. Ancient writings of scripture asked the question, "What does it prosper a man to gain the whole world yet lose his soul?" Likewise, I ask you, "How would any people prosper by gaining massive external success while ignoring and allowing the destruction of their body that is their temple?" When I committed to becoming a first-generation millionaire, I also made a personal commitment to be young and healthy enough to experience the benefits long before I passed my wealth onto my legacy and the generations beyond my earthly existence.

Holton told me to think about it a certain way, and his words really stuck with me. If you hurt a friend's feelings by saying something nasty or thoughtless, you can look him or her in the eye and sincerely apologize. That friend can forgive you, and you can go back to where you were before your comment. But if you smoke three packs a day for 20 years, you can't just apologize to your lungs and magically clean them up. You can't eat fried foods all your life and then apologize to your arteries and magically unclog them. That's not how this works. You have to do the work *now* to take care of your future self. It is the same for your education, in how you treat your mind, and how you treat the world around you. The ability to adjust, adapt, and sacrifice for the best interest of your future self is a major step toward mastering the mindset of a first-generation millionaire.

ACTION STEP

ook back at your goal from Pillar 4. Look back at your su-
persized goal from Pillar 8. Now, make a list of things you
need to do and make a list of things you need to not do because
they will interfere in your reaching your goal. For example, if
your goal is to have more money in your account at the end of
the month, you need to make a list of things you need to do to
reach that goal and a list of things you must stop doing because
they are in the way of your reaching that goal. Dinner out three
nights a week needs to go, but putting extra cash into a savings
account at the end of the week needs to be on the to-do list.

You won't be successful if you don't adjust your spending.
You have to do the work. For my health challenge, it was a "do"
to eat at least five servings of greens and a "do not" to skip a day
of exercise. It worked for me, and it will work for you. Be serious
about the list. Following the steps you outline for yourself is an
integral part of being a friend to your goals and your future self.

PILLAR 12

BECOMING A FRIEND TO YOUR FUTURE SELF—MENTALLY AND PHYSICALLY

EXAMINE WHAT YOU WANT AND WHAT IS HOLDING YOU BACK

Getting comfortable with taking action is a theme you'll see throughout this course. You must participate in your rescue.

Deliberate, strategic actions create real momentum and accelerate your pace toward your goals. That's why it's important to identify good action habits and counter-productive action habits.

Your Assignment

Create two lists:

1. Make a list of 10 things you will **start doing** that will complement your goal.

2. Make a list of 10 things you will **stop doing** because they are holding you back.

Examples

*Actions that **complement: Do**.*

- **Goal:** Quit smoking.

- **Action:** Get rid of all the cigarettes in the house.

*Actions that **hinder: Don't do.***

- **Goal:** Save $1,000 a month.

- **Action:** Don't go out to eat five times a week.

Now take a picture with the book and your filled-in answers, and tag me on Instagram and Twitter (@wimbrey), as well as on Facebook and LinkedIn. Share your progress and cheer on others!

Be sure to add our hashtags:

#BAMM

#WIMBREY

#CoachJohnny

PART IV
INSPECT WHAT YOU EXPECT

I n Pillar 10, we talked about taking inventory, which includes detailing every single part of your life and determining whether each part will help you reach your goals or stop you from reaching them. Now is your moment of honesty. Look at your goals from the beginning of this book. Are you inspecting what you expect? Are you pulling back the layers? Are you taking a self-inventory? Are you connecting the dots you need to follow to reach your goals? To make sure you are doing this and doing it in an effective way, we need to take a step back—and we'll do exactly that in Pillars 13, 14, and 15.

Staying in Position

They say success leaves clues, but so does failure. I can easily connect the dots to my success, *and* I can also connect the dots to my failures. Dwelling on your failures is never helpful but learning from them is. Here is an example from my personal life.

When I was 33, I—a man who had been committed to my family for a decade—decided that I wanted a divorce. It was my decision; it was my idea. We had been going through some rough patches, some family issues, and some in-law drama, and I decided I wanted out. I was subscribing to my failures, and I was participating in my failure. It was all my doing. I pushed for a 24-month separation and a more than $300,000 divorce that never even happened. After just 6 months of separation, we were already acting and living like a divorced couple. I did not want to save my marriage. I had lost 100 percent of hope.

But it was all pride. I had allowed several temporary moments to lead me to a permanent decision. I became a victim of not listening to my own message. There are plenty of marriages that have ended in justifiable divorces, but my decision to get a divorce was not justifiable based on our faith and belief system. I had no reason to even entertain the idea of divorce. Instead, we should have been investing in marital counseling and seminars, which would have saved me two years and hundreds of thousands of dollars in foolishness, turmoil, and pain. When I looked back, I could connect the dots to why it happened. It was clear; it was my pride and my ego. I can even connect the dots to my "aha" moment, that exact moment I realized that I was giving up on my number one commitment in my life.

Not everything is going to be perfect during your journey to your goal, but just as I did, you need to look back and take ownership. I can now recognize that my original desire to get a divorce was driven by my pride. I also know that it was my responsibility to inspect what I expected. *I* was the one who wanted to get married, *I* was the one who asked for the divorce, so *I* had to be the one to inspect my initial commitment and save my relationship. It's that simple.

Be authentic with yourself. Remember, you can always measure your character by the size of the obstacle that has derailed you. Look at the good and the bad. Look back at your failures. What was that obstacle? Why exactly did you drop that ball? I want you to build and challenge your character on this front. If you want to make it to the other side of your goal, you need to inspect what you expect and **stay in position**.

Anything that you are entertaining that has the potential to distract you from your goals is a clue that you are in danger of losing your position. Your position should always complement the direction of your expectations. Being out of position for a split second could allow someone else to reap the rewards of your past and current progress. Your ability or inability to master the art of understanding the power of your personal position will either cost you or make you millions. There is no in-between. Anything that you allow to alter your position from the direction of your personal goals or aspirations could lead to the death of your personal success. Position + Purpose = Destiny!

I had a hard time understanding what staying in position meant until I saw it acted out for me onstage. When I was 23, I attended a multiday leadership conference. I couldn't yet afford to pay for these conferences, so I served during the conference. I worked from seven o'clock in the morning to eleven o'clock at night, but this work allowed me to be in the small rooms and the big ones. I wasn't always comfortable doing the job, but I knew that it would pay off. That idea of staying in position was reinforced at this particular conference.

The keynote and guest speaker onstage asked for a volunteer. Eben Conner, who was actually my mentor at the time, volunteered and went up to the stage. The speaker told him to stand 30 feet in front of him, on the opposite side of the stage, and then he asked Eben to face him. We were all wondering what was going to happen next, especially Eben. Then the speaker said, "OK. I am a pitcher in a major league baseball game." His posture changed. He looked like he was getting ready to throw an imaginary ball to Eben. "Eben, you're the catcher."

Eben looked at the speaker, not quite knowing what to do next. And the speaker repeated, "Eben. I am a pitcher, and you are the catcher."

Eben smiled and raised his eyebrows, as if to say, "I heard you. What's next?"

The speaker repeated, "Eben, I'm the pitcher. You're the catcher. I'm on the mound, and you're on home plate."

Again, Eben's body language screamed, "So?"

"Who am I?" the speaker asked.

"You're the pitcher, sir." And the audience laughed.

"And who are you?"

"I'm the catcher."

The whole time this exchange was happening, the speaker was positioned to throw the ball. What Eben wasn't getting—what the audience was slowly realizing—was that the pitcher can't pitch unless the catcher is in position. The pitcher, one of the team's most important players, needs the catcher to be in position before he can do *anything*. Eben *finally* got it. "Oh!" He suddenly dropped down and got into a catcher's position. As soon as he got into position, the speaker "threw" the ball. By then, the lesson was learned.

It doesn't matter what your gift is if you are out of position. If you don't understand your position—if you don't know when to get into position, if you aren't ready to take your position at a moment's notice—you will never be able to play. It was in that moment that I understood the danger of not being in position and of not understanding what your position is. The whole world is waiting for you to get into position. And it's not just you who needs you in position. It is your team, your partners, and your future employees.

Take my business Wimbrey Training Systems as an example. I didn't start this company because I needed another stream of income. I created it to put myself in a position to employ others, pass along my knowledge to as many people as possible, and create a legacy for my children. Now I have employees who are thriving in this company. I have mentees who are creating their own businesses. And you, those who are reading this book right now. I got into position, and I am ready to stay in it for the long haul. Are you?

It all comes down to commitment. Imagine yourself as a sniper with your goal in the crosshairs. Keep your eye on the prize, and don't let anything distract you. Don't let anything take you out of position. And when you do get out of position (and you will), my question to you is this: How long will you allow yourself to stall before you get back into position? How long will you stay parked before you get back into action? Years and decades can go by before you choose to get back on the path to your goal. This happens to so many people out there. Don't let it happen to you.

Remember I said that one of the greatest lessons that Les Brown ever taught me was, "It is better to be prepared and never called than to be called and not be prepared." What I did not share with you is how frustrating it is being prepared and in position and having no idea *when or if* the call for opportunity will present itself.

But when the opportunity does present itself, that is when I want you to shine. I want you to be ready for it when it takes the corner and hits you smack in the face. Those who are organized and operating in their position—regardless of who's watching—deserve the call more than the people who get in position because they know the call is coming. Stay in position and make the *when*, the *where*, and the *how* none of your business. Your **preparation** plus your **position** will equal your **destiny**.

Here's a fun fact about me, Johnny Wimbrey. I'm not big on titles for myself. I respect and honor titles that people work hard to achieve, but I absolutely despise it when someone attempts to put a title on me with the intent to establish instant credibility. My wife and I have had very intense conversations about the subject. There are very powerful individuals with global celebrity influence in my life whom I love and honor who have passionately encouraged me to add a title to my name, and it breaks my heart to say no.

The truth is that if I said yes, it would take me out of position for the destiny that God himself has on my life. Chasing or accepting a title that would encourage or solidify why people should follow my teachings would be me selling out to my call and position. For the record, if you ever see me add an official title in front of my name, you can believe with 100 percent certainty that it was God himself who made that call and not a person, and I promise you even then I would go kicking and screaming. Why? Because position will always come before a title when it comes to my caring about how people see me. The moral to the story is if you want the call, get prepared. And if you desire to have a title, desire the position with an even greater passion than the title itself.

It is with extreme passion at this point in the book that you not only develop the first-generation-millionaire mindset but you also understand that getting there requires preparation and positioning. Continue to sharpen your axe, hone your skills, and stay in position for your destiny.

ACTION STEP

Think of something you set out to do and accomplished. What parts of your character made that success happen? What did you do to get there? Connect those dots, and look for patterns in your behavior and your character.

Now, go in the opposite direction. Think of a time you lost your position, took your eye off your goal, walked away, and never went back. Now write it down. What were the clues in your character that made you walk away? Connect the dots to why you left that goal behind. Do you see patterns in your life and in your character?

Just as you flexed the mental muscle of determining who is a friend or a foe—of who is an Instigator, Spectator, or Participator—I want you to flex the mental muscle of inspection. I want you to connect the dots of failure *and* connect the dots of success. I want you to put this practice into effect in *everything* you do. I want you to do this automatically. Without mastering the art of inspecting what you expect, you won't be able to master the focus you need to reach your goals. All successful people have the strength and faith to do this. You are no different.

PILLAR 13

STAYING IN POSITION
CONNECT THE DOTS

Self-inventory is critical when trying to map a plan for success. You need to be able to predict how you will react in a given situation **and** understand which reactions push you ahead or put you at risk.

This is your time to be **honest**. Account for your successes, and analyze your mistakes.

Your Assignment

Think about a time in the past when you **accomplished** a goal. Then, write down five actions you took that positioned you for success.

Next, think about a time when you **failed** to accomplish a goal. Write down five actions (or lack of action) on your part that kept you from achieving that goal.

Mission Accomplished (Goal): _____

Reasons for success:

1. _____

2. _____

3. _____

4. _____

5. _____

Mission Failed (Goal): _____

Reasons for failure:

1. _____

2. _____

3. _____

4. _____

5. _____

Now take a picture with the book and your filled-in answers, and tag me on Instagram and Twitter (@wimbrey), as well as on Facebook and LinkedIn. Share your progress and cheer on others!

Be sure to add our hashtags:

#BAMM

#WIMBREY

#CoachJohnny

Embracing Your New Points of No Return

I am sure that you have heard the term "point of no return" many times in your life. It means you are going to a place where you can't turn back, where going backward in your journey is not an option. Some people are afraid of the point of no return, but I want you to embrace it.

I want to stretch the possibilities of creating a new rule that you can immediately implement in your life using this very concept. This critical pillar is one of my core fundamental success principles, and it has changed my trajectory in life, leading me to become the businessman that I am today. Every single time I have progressed to a new level in life, I have established a new point that I can never return back to. Now we are getting into the nitty-gritty of inspecting what you expect. We've looked back, we've analyzed our character, and we've strengthened our commitment. Now it's time to plan out exactly what you need to do to reach your goal by the numbers.

Remember the coins in my pocket? When I was on a mission to make my first $100,000 year, I calculated exactly what I needed to do each week to reach that annual goal. I divided it by 52 weeks and saw that I needed to make $2,000 per week. In order to reach that, I knew that I had to set up 15 appointments per week. Out of those 15 appointments I made, I knew that I had to meet successfully with at least 8. And I knew that I had to make five sales to reach that number. Setting up 15 appointments a week meant two calls (and two coins) per day. Remember how we talked in Pillar 4 about goals and the rungs on the ladder to success? I wrote the rungs on my ladder and started climbing.

Doing the math is important, but it is only half of the equation (see what I did there?). The other half is creating your *point of no return* over and over again. When I was 22, I wanted to reach a new tier in my life. I knew what I wanted to do. I knew what I had to do to get to it. And I also knew that once I reached that point, it would be my point of no return. That meant that I could never go back to the life I had lived before I reached my most recent goal. This meant that I knew that I would always be climbing up the ladder. I never, ever wanted to reach a rung and then have to take a step back down. In my mind, each new goal that I reached became the new bottom rung—and I was never allowed back on that bottom step.

Every time I hit a new point of no return, I used that as a mental marker of what my minimal lifestyle would be. This meant different things to me at different times in my life. When I was first starting out, it was all about the numbers. Each rung in my ladder had a dollar amount next to it. At 22, that meant making $1,000 a week.

In order for me to do that, I had to trace the end result back to my weekly numbers. (It's a numbers game. We hear that phrase so often that we have turned it into a cliché, but it's true.) Not only do you need to know the numbers for your goal but you also need to know the numbers for your industry. Here was the plan for my industry at the time: Monday before 1:00 p.m. was my time to work the phones. Every Monday—without question—I spent 8:30 a.m. to 1:00 p.m. setting up my appointments for the week. If people I talked to during those hours wanted to see me right away, I would turn them down. I told them my first open appointment for any Monday was at 1:00 p.m. I was so structured and married to this mindset that despite having someone who wanted to see me that day, I knew the numbers for the week were more important than the right-now sale.

I started looking at the rungs on my ladder. I knew that I had to make at least 50 or more calls before 1:00 p.m. to set up 12 to 15 appointments for the week. I knew if I set up 12 appointments, I would meet with at least eight people. I knew if I saw eight people, I would sell to five of them. Five sales at an average of $200 per sale would put me at $1,000 per week after taxes. Once I hit a thousand per week, that was my new point of no return. I made $54,000 the year I turned 22. Earning that kind of money consistently from week to week became my new bottom rung. I knew exactly what I had to do to get there, so that plan became my bare minimum going forward.

Within the next 12 months, my brand-new house was built, the same year I got married, and I made a commitment to Crystal that she would never have to work. I also paid for her last year of college, paid off all her student loans, and made sure we were debt free before we had our first child.

I had created a time frame for what I wanted to accomplish, and I knew that neither I nor my wife could ever go backward. It was not just about the salary. I was not going to move Crystal to a smaller house or ask her to start working. It was about making sure we didn't owe money to anyone. I went above and beyond because my promise wasn't just to myself. It was to my current and future family as well. That year, living debt free and knowing that my wife would never work became my new bottom rung, my new point of no return. I knew I was never going to go backward in those two respects. I knew what I had to earn to have that life. Now I just had to keep climbing up.

When I was 25, the rungs on my ladder changed again. I had set my top rung for the end of the year as making an income that was double the amount that I had set only three years before. I decided my goal would be to make six figures by the end of the year. By then, I was selling onstage, promoting products, and selling insurance and security systems. I used those two coins in my pocket every day, set smaller 90-day goals, met them, and kept climbing that ladder. This time, however, I realized that I was climbing much more quickly than I had before.

By May 2000, I had made my $100,000 goal. I had given myself a year, and I achieved my goal in less than five months. After May, after I had already hit my top rung in less than half the time that I had allowed myself to hit it, I had no intention of slowing down. The pace I had been keeping to get there was my new point of no return. I was never going to work at a slower pace again.

I didn't take June to December off. I kept up that pace for the rest of the year. It was no longer about reaching that six-figure salary. It was about maintaining the earnings I had on a week-to-week basis. Earning $2,000 a week was my point of no return. I refused to slow down.

When I got to $250,000 per year, I knew I could never go back to less than $250,000 per year. That number was my new point of no return. When I got to $1 million per year, I knew I would never go back to less than $1 million per year. *That* was my new point of no return.

As soon as I hit each new number, that number became my new point of no return. Some years, the change in income levels was smaller than the change in other years, but there was always an increase; there was always a change. I want you to have that mentality now too. The goal at the top of the ladder can be amended as circumstances change and you grow in experience and broaden your perspective, but I never, ever want you to slide down the ladder. I never want you to take a step down. Every time you hit a goal, that goal becomes your base. That is your new point of no return.

From purely a financial perspective, constantly creating *new points of no return* is one of my most important rules when it comes to year-over-year income. The most incredible thing about adopting this principle is that you are competing only with **your** previous success. And the amazing thing about the principle is that it's not hard to accept the fact that you can do something again that you have already accomplished and push for just a little bit more. It's a friendly competition between you and your previous year.

Having and keeping to a point of no return is a key element in my life that creates perpetual success. You will never become a first-generation millionaire if you hit your very first goal and just stop. Set your goal, do the math, and reach it. Then set an even higher goal. This book is designed to create personal accountability by your never being passive with yourself when it comes to being OK with going backward. For over 15 consecutive years, I have never gone backward when it comes to a year-after-year financial increase. I credit that to the simple fact that I can never go backward once I've established a new point of no return.

What started out as a personal principle in my life has now become a Wimbrey Financial Law that is a major contributor to mastering the mindset of a first-generation millionaire. As your coach during this journey, it is my desire that you implement this law by scratching off my last name in "Wimbrey Financial Law" and replacing it with your last name and that you teach your new law to your children with the hopes that they will pass it down to their children and beyond.

ACTION STEP

Think back to a time when you moved backward in your life. How did you approach your goals back then? How did you go about reaching them? What happened when you didn't reach them? Or what happened when you found yourself taking a step down the rungs on your ladder or staying on one rung for much too long? Use this as the inspiration for what *not* to do going forward. Write down where you went wrong and how to fix that in the future.

Next, think back to each of these instances, and write out all the excuses you have given yourself (and others) when they happened. How did you justify your downward trajectory? Did you blame a boss, a spouse, a child? Did you blame your education level? Your parents? Your upbringing? Keep this list handy because you will be using that list in this pillar's assignment.

PILLAR 14

EMBRACING YOUR NEW POINTS
OF NO RETURN

REPLACE YOUR EXCUSES
WITH SOLUTIONS

You've set your goals, and you've done the math on how to get there. You know that your only direction is forward. Each time you hit a goal, that is your new **point of no return**.

Your Assignment

- Take the excuses you wrote down after you finished reading this chapter.

- Focus on the ones you can change. If it was a toxic work environment, how can you address this problem so that it won't keep you from moving forward? If it was an unsupportive spouse, what conversations can you have to put him or her at ease? If it was an issue with your education, how can you earn the degree you need for what you want to do?

- Add these solutions to your list of goals. Keep this list handy so that if you find yourself making the same excuses again, you have a go-to list of responses to squash them before they can stop you from moving forward.

Now take a picture with the book and your filled-in answers, and tag me on Instagram and Twitter (@wimbrey), as well as on Facebook and LinkedIn. Share your progress and cheer on others!

Be sure to add our hashtags:

#BAMM

#WIMBREY

#CoachJohnny

Eating off One Plate at a Time

One of the misconceptions about personal development is that the more information you have, the better off you will be. That is a fallacy. In actuality, the more laser focused you are on certain information that complements where you want to go—even if it's less information—the more successful you will be.

I cannot stress enough the importance of staying focused. In order to talk about staying focused and in position, let's talk about something unexpected: food. I love food. There is nothing like the joy and satisfaction of a well-prepared meal. Let's pretend that I love all types of foods so much that I decide to go to all of these restaurants on the same day. Soul, Mexican, Thai, Indian, Italian. I eat it all. The reality is that even if they are all five-star, high-quality restaurants, there is a 100 percent chance that I'm going to get sick. No matter how much I love it and want it, my body will start to reject the food. Even though the chefs at these restaurants may be at the top of their game and each dish is tastier than the last, I will *never* be able to enjoy all these restaurants in one day.

The same thing applies to learning new languages. If you're struggling to learn five different languages at the exact same time, it's because you're focusing on too many languages and alphabets and vocabularies at once. Learn one well and then learn another and then another. The danger of learning too many things at one time leads to chaos because you aren't able to give all your attention to one thing. You have to take time to digest it. You have to take time to appreciate it. To savor it. If you don't, all that time and money you've spent will be wasted.

If you find yourself a victim to having too many self-development approaches, too many seminars, and too many voices in your head, I want you to slow down. Look down at your table. If you spend all your time and energy trying to absorb as many lessons as you can without actually being able to apply those lessons and see real change in your life, chances are, you are eating off too many plates at once. Take a step back and look at where you want to be in the moment and where you want to be in the near future. The rest can wait until you are able to focus on those two points.

For example, say you want to learn about leadership, how to invest in the stock market, how to manage employees, and how to grow your business. Of course, all of those are important, but only one is important now. If you are starting your own business, read about how to be a better CEO. Own that information while knowing that the next thing you need to know is how to manage your new employees. Your employees don't care how you invest in the stock market. They don't care how you are going to grow a business you just started. They care about your being the best CEO you can be and then being the best boss to them you can be. Sometimes you don't even have to read an entire book to get what you need out of it. Pick and choose the chapters that apply, and go back to the other parts when you need them.

Holton Buggs has a unique way of looking at this idea. He told me once to think of a grocery store. When you go food shopping, you don't go up and down the aisles, putting literally everything you see in your cart, right? That would be insane. You know what you want to eat, you make a list of what you need, and you buy just that and nothing else. You don't get distracted and buy everything in the butcher's window, every bag of chips, every type of fruit, and then every brand of pet food when you don't even have a pet. Treat your mind like that grocery cart. Only take what you know you need, and leave everything else behind.

In order to really bring this visual home, I want you to imagine a funnel. Google the image if you have to. Anything that goes into the funnel has to complement your goal. Anything that has nothing to do with your goal *cannot* go into the funnel. If you stuff too many things in the narrow head of the funnel, it will get blocked. Not only will you not be able to do the things you need to do well, but you won't even be able to do the extra things well either. It's a lose-lose situation all around.

How can your goals make it through to the other side if the funnel is blocked? If your main goal is to be a writer but you also have a dog-walking business, a child-care business, and a meal-delivery service, I will tell you right now that you will never be a writer. The dogs, and the kids, and the food packages are clogging up your funnel. Not only will your writing career never take off, but you won't even be able to focus on one job to make it lucrative. You will never be able to give any of these four things your everything because there are too many plates on your table. There are too many items in your grocery cart. There are too many things clogging your funnel.

Go inside your funnel, and pluck out anything that goes against your main goal. Go back to your lists from Pillars 5, 11, and 13. What foes might you have overlooked because they were disguised as productivity? If multiple businesses are pulling you out of position, they need to come out of the funnel. Anything that takes your goal out of your crosshairs needs to go. Take the temporary loss for the ultimate gain.

ACTION STEP

Write down everything you are doing that's complementing where you want to go. If your goal is to master a certain skill, write down all the ways you are going to master that one skill. If your goal is to open a certain type of business, write down all the ways you are going to open that business.

The point of this exercise is to make your main goal your main source of income. Everything after that is extra. Say you want to become a master chef, for example, but your essential income is from a lawn mowing company. If this is the case, you now have to prioritize. If mowing lawns is taking away from becoming a chef, you have to eliminate that stream of income. "But, Johnny," you may ask, "if the point of this book is to become a first-generation millionaire, *why* would I eliminate income?"

If your goal is to become a chef and you are unable to meet that goal because you are mowing lawns, then the lawn mowing is taking you away from your goal. It's as simple as that. Remember, the very thing that is producing could be distracting you from your goal. Sometimes, you have to give up to get up. If you focus on becoming a chef, finding success in that field, and making the money you set out to make, you can then add the lawn mowing back in as an extra stream of income if you need to.

Every significant level of increase that I have ever accomplished in my life was directly attached to my ability to sacrifice and leave behind something that was holding me back in life. If I found I was eating off two plates at the same time, I pushed one plate aside and focused on the other with all my energy.

To this day, I eliminate any and everything that has the potential of hindering my progress as soon as I identify it as a foe to my goals. There are things in my life that I have eliminated for a season, but there are also things in my life that I have eliminated permanently, with zero chances of return. **When I let those things go, I know that I am participating in my own rescue.** In doing so, I know I am going from generational poverty to ultimately establishing myself as a first-generation millionaire.

PILLAR 15

EATING OFF ONE PLATE AT A TIME
STAY IN POSITION AND AVOID THE SIDE HUSTLES

A distraction doesn't always take the form of a foe. Sometimes when you stretch yourself too thin, you end up getting in the way of your primary goals.

At this moment, you need **laser focus**. Someone with a one-track mind is more likely to reach the finish line than someone who's juggling multiple projects.

It's time to **clear the path**.

Your Assignment

Access all of your revenue streams.

Eliminate any project or side hustle that's **pulling you out of position** to reach your primary goal. Leave the ones that keep you on a **productive path** toward wealth.

List all of your **revenue streams**. Then decide which ones you will maintain and which ones you will eliminate.

Revenue Streams	Maintain	Eliminate

Now take a picture with the book and your filled-in answers, and tag me on Instagram and Twitter (@wimbrey), as well as on Facebook and LinkedIn. Share your progress and cheer on others!

Be sure to add our hashtags:

#BAMM

#WIMBREY

#CoachJohnny

PART V
EXECUTE VERSUS EXCUSE

Excuses and execution are two sides of the same coin. Whiners excuse, and winners execute. Whiners have mastered the art of excuses. They always have an explanation for why they are losing. Winners simply execute and win. There is no spectrum; there is no in-between. Remember, this is a book for people who will become first-generation millionaires, not for people who are simply trying to.

Executing Instead of Excusing

You can either become a master at making excuses and procrastinating or a master at putting a plan into action and following through with your intentions. I want to encourage you to subscribe to the mindset of someone who executes a plan. Do you want to be a *goal setter* or a *goal getter*? Do you want to see results, not just activity?

If you want to make excuses, you will live in the land of those who finish before they even start. That is not where first-generation millionaires live. They decide to do something, figure out how to do it, and follow through. When things get off course due to circumstances outside of your control, you need to know how to get back on track without making excuses to yourself and to others.

I'm not saying that there aren't opportunities for explanations. But when you explain what went wrong, you have to tell the truth. You are going to have to explain your mistakes or your team's mistakes to someone one day. The trick is to make sure it's honest. Don't embellish, don't blame others, and don't make excuses. You will get nowhere fast if you fill up your tank with excuses.

We all make mistakes. Making a mistake doesn't make us bad or good. It makes us human. When you do make a mistake, go through the following process to get everything back on track:

First: Own it. Acknowledge the mistake. Don't ignore it. The absolute fastest way to self-sabotage is personal denial.

Then: If it is a public mistake, seek wisdom immediately. Get help in orchestrating your response, and make sure your path of correction is very clear while extending your personal remorse and commitment to fixing the problem. Do not allow any time to go by to allow anyone to dictate a false narrative.

Lastly: Offer something to make up for your mistake because doing so will build trust. Then overdeliver on your offer. Remember, trust is a voluntary bridge that people have to want to cross. Your offering a bonus or free gift and overdelivering is an invitation to return and cross over your bridge of trust.

Doing this will help others restore their confidence in you and the goal you are working to accomplish. If you simply make excuses and walk away, you will leave room for a false narrative to be dictated by anyone motivated to share their opinions. Remember, perception wins over facts in the short run. To win back people's trust, show remorse, offer a plan and a promise to remedy the problem, and overdeliver on that promise. When things go off course, you need to know how to get them back on. You need to form a plan and execute it. Excuses will get you nowhere.

Making excuses to others when something goes awry is one thing. But what about the excuses you make to yourself? What happens when you find yourself stuck in a cycle of complacently wandering away from the path you set for yourself? Do you try to justify why you aren't meeting your goals? These excuses and justifications are foes to your goals. Facing the truth about yourself can be hard, but doing so means you are participating in your own rescue, and you are making sure that your actions and attitudes are in the friends category.

I hear my clients give me excuses all the time:

"It wasn't my fault!" or "I couldn't finish because life got in the way and I could not find the time!" or even "My car broke down. What was I supposed to do?"

When you find yourself making excuses for your lack of progress, I want you to return to Parts I and III. I want you to revisit your goals. Find your goal ladder. What rung are you on? If you aren't on the ladder anymore, why not? What in your life took you away from the goals you set for yourself?

Then, I want you to take an inventory of your choices and your actions. Remember, these excuses you are making to yourself are your goal's foes. Think carefully about why you are making them. Are the excuses you are making now helping your future self? Of course, they aren't. If that's the case, why the hell are you making them?

You can master the art of execution and be truthful about what is happening during your moments of setback, or you can be a master of giving excuses. But you can't execute and give excuses at the same time. Now is the time to build your character by learning how to execute your plans and to give honest explanations if those plans go south.

——

You are the only one who decides whether you are going to give up and make excuses about it or execute your dream and participate in your own rescue. Most people decide to execute a plan based on dramatic situations. My mother quit smoking because she thought she had cancer. My father quit drinking because his doctor told him if he didn't, drinking would lead to a certain death. I want you to decide to execute not because you want your life to *continue* as it has been but because you want to *launch* your new life.

You have the potential, you have the drive, and now you have the character to build yourself into a first-generation millionaire. Commit to yourself, solidify your faith, know your value. Make it happen.

ACTION STEP

f you are willing to lie to yourself, you will never master wealth. Be honest with yourself. I want you to write down the reasons you have skipped certain assignments in this book. Don't look shocked! If I were a betting man, I would say that you have probably skipped at least one of the assignments, or you simply did not give it 100 percent, which means you cut corners. Remember, this is your life not mine. If you have skipped assignments, now is the time to look at why you did so and then go back and complete them.

By cutting corners when you begin your journey, you are cutting down your own character. Without a strong character in place, you will never be able to achieve and maintain the first-generation-millionaire mindset. The more times you cut corners, the more times you give excuses, the more times you don't participate in your own rescue, the more times you don't inspect what you expect, the more likely it is that you will form the character of someone who is good at giving excuses, at reacting, at embellishing why he or she is failing.

True character is who you are when no one is around. You can act however you want in front of other people, but if you lie to yourself over and over and over again, soon you will have nothing but lies. That is not the foundation of a first-generation millionaire. You can take my word for it, or you can learn it the hard way.

I recommend that you look back at where you cut corners in this book, figure out why, write down those reasons, and then complete the assignments you missed. Once those are done, you can turn the page.

PILLAR 16

EXECUTING INSTEAD OF EXCUSING
ELIMINATE EXCUSES TO
ALLOW FOR SUCCESS

Setting goals is **critical** to success. Accomplishing goals **is success.**

You already know the journey will be challenging. If it weren't challenging, you'd already have what you want. Once you set a goal, you must be unrelenting.

Even when a ball is dropped, winners are able to assess honestly and provide candid explanations. This quality is a game changer because it promotes learning and growth.

Your Assignment

Find out if your **natural instinct** is to make excuses or provide explanations.

At some point today, you will have had the opportunity to either make an excuse or practice humility and give an explanation.

Below, describe that moment and how you handled it:

_____

_____

_____

_____

_____

_____

Now take a picture with the book and your filled-in answers, and tag me on Instagram and Twitter (@wimbrey), as well as on Facebook and LinkedIn. Share your progress and cheer on others!

Be sure to add our hashtags:

#BAMM

#WIMBREY

#CoachJohnny

Banishing Your Inner Try-Baby

Now that you are being honest with yourself, now that you are ready to take execution to the next level, I want to talk seriously about "try-babies." People who justify their failures with excuses—"I tried! I tried my best!"—will never see the success they want. Today is the first day that the word *try* is now banished from your vocabulary forever. There is no value in that word. It does nothing for you. You are either doing something, or you are not doing something. "Trying" is useless. As Yoda said, "Do or do not. There is no try." If you want to participate in your own rescue, you have to actually do so.

Going forward, replace "try" with "do my best." You can lie to yourself when you say "try," but you know in your heart what your best is. You also know what it isn't. You will never adapt and change without a moral connection. You know that it is never OK morally to lie to yourself. Even if you don't do your best, you can at least accept the fact that there was more you could have done. Apply that lesson to next time. Shrugging and saying, "Well, I tried" will never get you anywhere.

Right after I graduated from high school, I was accepted into a two-year collegiate acting program. Every day, I would wake up and drive an hour from Fort Worth to Dallas in the worst traffic imaginable. But I did it every morning because I wanted to be an actor. I applied. I auditioned. I found a way to pay for it. This school was my decision. That was something that I subscribed to, so it was my job to participate in making it happen, no matter the cost.

I was 19 years old when I was making this drive, and it wasn't in a BMW convertible, I can tell you that. It was my old beat-up 1988 Hyundai that I had bought myself my senior year in high school. My car leaked oil nonstop, so every 20 miles or so, I had to pull over, pop the hood, and pour oil into the car to keep it going. On the morning of a particularly important showcase, my car was leaking oil as usual. Drip, drip, drip. And just as it had every other morning, my oil light indicated low oil. But this time was different. I pulled over, and as I rushed to fill up the oil, I managed to spill a little on the overheated engine. Suddenly, the engine went up in flames. As quickly as I could, I ran to the back of the car, popped the trunk back open, and pulled out a blanket. I used the blanket to put out the fire, got back into the car, and drove the rest of the way to school for the showcase.

Why did I go to such lengths—especially dangerous ones—to get to school? I did it because I was the one who said I wanted to be an actor. I was the one who said I wanted to go to this school and complete this program. I was participating in what I said I wanted to do. Why didn't I just call and say, "My car is on fire on the side of the road. I can't come in today"? (Because you really don't get a better excuse than that.) Who wouldn't have given me a free pass? Me. I wouldn't have bought it. I knew that I could still go forward, so I did.

Take a break from reading for a minute, and pick up a pencil. Hold it up in the air. Now try to drop it. What happened? If the pencil fell, how can you say you *tried* to drop it? You dropped it. You did it. There was no "trying" to drop the pencil. You were either holding it, or it was on the floor or wherever it landed. There was nothing in between. You see, the word *try* has absolutely no meaning.

I've now trained myself to cringe at the word *try*. It doesn't have a tangible definition. Saying you will "try" is just a preemptive excuse for potential failure. My kids even correct me when I say the word *try*—and they correct themselves. I urge you to take this even one step further. If you simply take the word out of your vocabulary, you aren't necessarily ridding yourself of that mindset. You have to hold yourself accountable in the now by making sure that when you put effort into something, you can honestly say you did your best or you can own up to the fact that you didn't. **If you aren't ready to stop being a try-baby, then you aren't ready to be a first-generation millionaire.** It's that simple.

Most of us practice our excuses so much that we buy our own explanations, even if they aren't honest. You will never be a millionaire if you buy your own excuse for giving up. I don't want you to *try* to finish this book and all the assignments. I want you to *do it*. I want to hear about your massive successes, not about how you tried to make it happen and failed. Eliminate the word *try* from your vocabulary. You can't have execution and excuses at the exact same time. The word *try* is a premeditated excuse for a future failure. Try-baby? Or do-baby? Mastering the mindset and becoming a first-generation millionaire is reserved for those who do, not for those who try.

ACTION STEP

Implement something that you said you were going to *try* to do. Start that book on your bedside table, call that dream mentor, create a new way of doing things in your office. Write down what you *tried* to do. Then execute it. Implement something that you have been *trying* to do. Share it with your community.

Go from being an Instigator to a Participator in the very thing you have been talking about for a long time. Don't come back to the book until it is finished.

PILLAR 17

BANISHING YOUR INNER TRY-BABY

TAKE ACTION IMMEDIATELY AND UNLEASH YOUR CONFIDENCE

The biggest lie you tell yourself in pursuit of a goal is, "I'll do it next time." No, you won't. If you take nothing else from this course, know this: **the time is now**—because that's all there is.

You either do it now, or you don't. Excuses are for whiners and try-babies. Winners do. They don't try.

Start doing. Right now.

Your Assignment

I want you to implement something that you have talked about doing but haven't yet. Today is the day.

Pick a project, a goal, a new habit—and **do it**.

What do you want to implement?

_____

_____

_____

Describe the actions you took:

_____

_____

_____

Now take a picture with the book and your filled-in answers, and tag me on Instagram and Twitter (@wimbrey), as well as on Facebook and LinkedIn. Share your progress and cheer on others!

Be sure to add our hashtags:

#BAMM

#WIMBREY

#CoachJohnny

Getting off Your "But"

've heard it all: "I want to be successful, *but* . . ." "I want to lose weight, *but* . . ." "I want to stop smoking, *but* . . ." It's time to get off your "buts." Let me give you an example that changed my life dramatically. My decision to get off my "but" in this instance is the reason I was able to set up businesses around the globe, make over $1 billion in revenue in the last decade, and write this book today. If I had let this "but" get in the way, who knows where I would be.

A few years after I joined forces with Les Brown, I began to tell people that I wanted to take my speaking career to an international stage. As soon as I said it, I knew it was my responsibility to make it happen. I told everyone who would listen that I was going to be an international speaker by the end of the year. It was my responsibility to stay in position and to prepare for the call. It was my responsibility to take my local message and expand my abilities and enhance my skills so that I could relate to an international audience.

Soon after I started ramping up my outreach, I got a phone call from an event organizer in London: "Johnny," he said to me, "I may have something for you. There is a seminar coming up: 'The Mind of an Entrepreneur' in London. They are looking for three or four American speakers, and they love you. I showed them who you are, and they just love you. But here's the thing: It's a showcase, so you will only have 10 minutes. And you have to pay your own travel expenses including your own hotel."

In essence, what he was offering me was the equivalent of my paying them for the opportunity to speak to their audience. Paying to appear is a game I told myself I would never play as a professional speaker. I wanted to explain to him that I was becoming a big deal in America. People were paying me well, I was gaining a strong reputation, and I had just written a book. I had been working my tail off, and now someone was asking me to work for free.

Les Brown pulled me aside and told me that it would diminish my future value to take this offer. In addition to Les's concerns, I wondered to myself why would I want to pay for my own plane ride and hotel to work for free, giving up money I could be making at home? My wife also had reservations about the invitation. A lot of our money had gone into the book I had just written, and we weren't seeing a return on it yet. Money was a bit tight, and she was worried that it would be even tighter if I left a sure thing here in America for a risk overseas.

I listened to both of them, and I said, "I told you I wanted to be an international speaker; here is my chance. The door is open. I need to kick it down." So I went. At that time my mother-in-law worked for American Airlines, and I traveled standby and booked the cheapest hotel I could. When I got to London, I was overwhelmed. It was a full day of events, and there were news cameras everywhere. All these successful people were milling around as if it was nothing. I brought my box of books and audio coaching programs to sell, just hoping to break even.

"Johnny," the program directors said when I arrived, "we want to use you last because we like your energy, and you will end things on a high note." That's fine, I thought. As long as I get my ten minutes. Well, the speaker before me went over his allotted time by five minutes, and after the transition and introductions, I wound up being left with only three and a half minutes. But I was there. I was about to step onto an international stage—and I was doing exactly what I said I was going to do.

I was surrounded by British people, many of whom can be very reserved. As I was wrapping up my speech, however, my stomach dropped. I had forgotten to talk about my product. I had been holding my product in my hand the entire three minutes, but I had gotten so caught up in fulfilling my purpose of serving the people that I forgot to also serve my own agenda. I never mentioned anything about my product or services, the sales of which would have actually paid for this trip.

After I finished speaking, I noticed that the energy in the room was totally different than it had been before I spoke. The Brits were standing up, and they were clapping. As I exited the stage, they followed me, oblivious to the fact that the emcees were still wrapping things up. Walking in a very fast pace toward my product table, cursing under my breath, I expected to see the few people who had liked my truncated speech. I was shocked to find that the line at my table was out the door. I sold double the amount of product I thought I would sell, and I paid for the trip twice over. At the end of the trip, I was an international speaker. I did what I said I was going to do.

After I got back home, I didn't hear anything from the "Mind of an Entrepreneur" organizers for months. Then, a month before their next conference was taking place, I got another phone call. The "Mind of an Entrepreneur" was holding an event again in London, and the organizers were reaching out to see if I could come. The call was a little different this time around though.

"They want to bring you in. They want you to be the keynote speaker. They are going to set up a television interview for you. And they want you to speak on the panel that will include local billionaires and celebrities to answer questions. They will pay for your trip and hotel, and you can sell as much product as you want. What do you say?"

I went. I did the interviews. I gave the keynote speech. The lines were out the door for my products. But more importantly, someone in the audience heard what I was saying, saw my energy, and reached out to me personally. This person brought me back to England less than two weeks later, where I spearheaded an entrepreneurship course. Another someone saw the work that I did there and asked me to join him in an international business venture. That very same venture launched my career into the $100 million powerhouse it is today.

At the start of this story, all I did was agree to a ten-minute speech, which turned into a three-and-a-half-minute speech. I seized the chance when it was presented to me. It's a moment I will look back on with awe and humility. That moment turned into $100 million in revenue in more than 50 countries. Because of that speech, I became everything I wanted to be: a successful speaker, a business owner, and a philanthropist. It is the reason I am a first-generation millionaire.

If, however, my response to that first phone call had been, "But I'm making good money here," or "But I would never work for free," or "But what will happen if I fail?" I could have lost the opportunity to earn everything I have today. I got off my "but" and changed my entire life.

As a business coach, one of the hardest things for me to do is get clients to **believe** that they can accomplish something that they have **never** done before. Many times, we allow our crippling beliefs to stagnate our possibilities because we simply have a hard time believing we can go past what we have already done. In most cases, I would have to use examples of *other people* who had set out to accomplish something and ultimately achieved what they had set out to do. We use others' testimonies as the motivating factors.

So many times, when we set out on a mission to accomplish a new journey, we typically are motivated by the success of someone else's story, someone who has accomplished the exact same thing for the first time. The Roger Bannister story is an incredible an example. He was the first individual to ever break the four-minute mile on record.

As a matter of fact, doctors and other healthcare professionals warned people against even attempting the four-minute mile because of the dangers that an athlete's heart might explode as well as sustaining many other physical injuries. In 1954, Roger Bannister would break the record proving the professionals wrong. But here's what's more interesting. His record was broken just 46 days later. Within a few years, hundreds of people would break his record. Today, it's in the thousands. It's as if one man gave us permission to cross a barrier that professionals told athletes was impossible. Sometimes giving yourself permission to succeed is all you need to invite others into your new promised land.

For me, my goal of becoming a first-generation millionaire was basically my saying that I wanted to break a record in my family name. There was no evidence for me to follow. There were no examples for me to lean on in my family. But I met my goal. I believe that being the first one in my family to master the art of having a millionaire mindset will lead to hundreds and eventually thousands in the future who will follow me beyond the barrier that has never been achieved before. I want you to give yourself permission to break a record, to be the first, to establish a new point of no return for generations to come. Waiting for someone else to be first is a crippling mindset, and it is the exact opposite of the mindset of the first-generation millionaire.

To overcome this crippling mindset:

1. You **must** give yourself permission to be the first.

2. You **must** get off any "but" that you are allowing to hold you back.

3. You **must** become your own authority of what you see yourself accomplishing.

I've heard so many excuses as to why clients thought they couldn't be the first to accomplish something. They would tell me, "I'm too young," "I'm too old," or "I'm from the wrong side of the tracks." It was frustrating to me to see them already giving up before they made a move. To every excuse, I would say exactly what Les Brown told me when I came to him full of excuses: "Johnny, if you continue to argue for your limitations, I'm going to allow you to keep them, and our relationship is over." It made them realize that climbing up the ladder and having that point-of-no-return mindset was the only way they were going to reach their goals.

Think back to the work you have already done. In Pillar 6, you created a plan just in case life throws you a curve ball, and in Pillar 12, you learned how to become a friend to your future self. You already have that forward-thinking mindset. Now is the time to put that into action. Move up. Move forward. You will never achieve that millionaire mindset until that is your only direction.

ACTION STEP

R ead the following questions, and answer them honestly. Write down your answers. It's just you and you now. Be as honest as possible:

Why did you buy this book?

Why have you read to the end?

Why do you want to be wealthy?

Why do you want to take your life to the next level?

My WHY is to empower every one of you to reach your full potential. I want you to experience greatness. This reason—this mission—is going to outlive me. Your success is my success. Now that you are turning the corner to finishing this book and you have invested time, resources, and energy in your future, you are a part of this movement. Thank you for helping me reach my goal, which is to expose the mindset that creates first-generation millionaires.

Before moving on to the absolutely mandatory conclusion, have an honest conversation with yourself about why you are doing this. Once you have your WHY in writing, start your journey. If the door cracked open today, would you have the courage to kick it open all the way?

Find that WHY. I promise you, the door is going to crack. Do the work. Build the pillars of your character. Be prepared for when you are called.

PILLAR 18

GETTING OFF YOUR "BUT"
WHAT IS YOUR WHY?

Problem plus solution equals **opportunity**. However, if you're able to invent new paths forward *before* there's an urgency to do so, you'll uncover greatness. The nature of your motivation determines which kind of problem solver you'll become.

What is your **WHY?** You need to know what it is because it will outlive you.

Your Assignment

I want you to understand your **driving motivations**. Be honest with yourself, and answer these questions:

Why *did you invest in this book?*

_____

_____

_____

_____

Why *did you make it to the end?*

_____

_____

_____

_____

Why *are you allowing me to be your coach?*

_____

_____

_____

_____

Now, for the last time, take a picture with the book and your filled-in answers, and tag me on Instagram and Twitter (@wimbrey), as well as on Facebook and LinkedIn. Share your success, and learn from the success of your peers!

Be sure to add our hashtags:

#BAMM

#WIMBREY

#CoachJohnny

Conclusion

My first memory is of being denied milk in a homeless shelter. Later in life, I failed the second grade. After that, my mother left me with my alcoholic father. In high school, I made some of the worst decisions of my life—decisions that led to a felony arrest. The statistics don't lie. I should be in prison with my brother. Or dead like so many of my friends. Or living a life of violence in a gang.

Based on all the studies about someone who has gone through what I have and is also an African-American man only a few generations out of slavery, I shouldn't be a millionaire. I shouldn't be in a happy, committed marriage. I shouldn't own the businesses I own. I shouldn't drive the cars I drive or earn the money I make. But I do. By the grace of God and my dedication to my work, I beat those numbers; I beat those statistics. I chose not to participate in what society expected of me. I became a first-generation millionaire because I refused to let someone else's opinion about me become my reality.

The abusive father wasn't my fault. The shelter wasn't my fault. The unstable mother wasn't my fault. Those were all out of my control. But what I did have control over was the fact that I smoked weed and drank alcohol as a child. I had control over where and with whom I was spending my time in middle school and in high school too. And I had control over the choices that led to my arrest.

The fact is, I participated in my downfall. I was the one who got me into the hole, so in the end, I had to be the one to get me out. I couldn't just climb out though. Climbing out would only bring me to the edge of the hole. No, I had to slingshot myself out. I needed to pour on 10 times the effort—or 100 times the effort, or 1,000—whatever it took—to get me out and as far away from that hole as possible.

When you pull back a slingshot, you are creating friction and adversity. You need to put all of your energy into pulling the object backward. It doesn't want to go where you are pulling it—away from gravity, away from its natural comfort zone— and it will fight you every step of the way. But if you pull it back to just before the slingshot breaks, think of how far it can go. There is no friction, nothing holding it back, as it sails toward its new goal.

I *had* to slingshot myself out. And I did. I went from being a teenage felon to a millionaire in less than a decade. Only a decade has passed since I made my first million dollars, and now I speak all over the world, I oversee a global distribution team that is worth over $100 million a year in production, and I have reached almost every goal I have set out to achieve. In another 10 years, I will be conquering goals I don't even have yet.

How was all this possible? How did I manage to slingshot myself so far and so fast? Simple. **I participated in my own rescue.** Just as I did, you must also accept the fact that it is all up to you. There will be people who complement your success, but you have to be the one who puts in more energy, time, and effort than anyone else. Only you can stop yourself. Only you can make it happen.

Becoming a first-generation millionaire is not a personal best for me. I didn't make my first million and then just stop. Success like this was never a goal for me. It was never a destination. Success—becoming a millionaire, owning my own businesses, speaking on the world stage—will always be a direction. My father was a trash-man. My grandfather spent his life on the run after killing a white man who was attempting to kill him. My ancestors were slaves. I'm only a few generations outside of slavery, but here I am, a multimillionaire, teaching others around the world how to do what I've done. And my daughters, Psalms and Hannah, and my son, Honor, will be more successful than I am. I know it.

Becoming a first-generation millionaire is not a trophy I put on my shelf. It is part of the journey to where I am still headed. I have no idea where I will end up, but I know I am very far from where I started. I want this exact journey for you too. Don't rest once you reach your first goal. Use that success as a stop on the way to something even greater.

Understand that becoming the first millionaire in your family is not a destination. It's a direction. You cannot stand still, no matter what. You are either progressing or regressing. There is no in-between. If you stand still while the world moves around you, you will only move backward. Keep coming back to the lessons in this book to set new goals and reach them. You have unlimited potential. Once it is unleashed, there are no limits to what you can do.

Index

Meet Johnny

Johnny Wimbrey is an author, speaker, trainer, and motivator, working with sales teams, high-profile athletes, politicians, and personalities around the world. Since leaving behind a world of drugs and crime at 18, Johnny has launched three companies (Wimbrey Training Systems, Wimbrey Global, and Royal Success Club International). Today he heads a sales team of thousands in more than 30 countries, overseeing an active customer database of half a million families.

He has coauthored and contributed to several motivational books, including *Conversations on Success: 6 Thought Leaders Redefine What It Means to Succeed* and *Multiple Streams of Inspiration*. From his bestselling book *From the Hood to Doing Good* to his instructional guides for achieving success, Johnny's written works further demonstrate his ability to change people's lives through his words.

Johnny continues to traverse the globe, sharing his powerful message through speaking engagements and products. His incredible rags-to-riches story has resonated with audiences all over the world, from Africa to Australia, India to Italy, Sweden to Spain. His unique high-energy style has made him an incredibly sought-after speaker, and he has shared the stage with legendary personal development gurus such as Les Brown and the late greats Jim Rohn and Zig Ziglar, just to name a few. His blunt honesty motivates people to stop thinking and start doing.